Let My People Go

Let My People Go

True story of how to overcome
sexual perversion.

Alvin Mukisa

To order additional copies of this book, contact:
Xlibris
844-714-8691
www.Xlibris.com
Orders@Xlibris.com
840062

CONTENTS

INTRODUCTION

For twelve years, I was a Christian minister of the gospel in a Pentecostal church, and everything seemed perfect. However, I was struggling with pornography and masturbation as a young man. I frequently visited a cyber café to feed my desire for pornography. This seemed fitting; however, unknown to me was the strong bondage I was creating.

Cyber cafes are commercial places where people get internet access for a cost. One day, at a café', a young man of my age bracket sat next to my station and was watching homosexual pornography. This seemed more attractive than the heterosexual pornography I was watching. We instantly connected when I inquired from him the website he was visiting. After leaving the café, I took a while, watching this porn until I became addicted and sought sexual relations with that guy since I had retained his contact.

As a Christian, I felt convicted and realized that I was bound in a sinful lifestyle, which I needed to end immediately. I tried several options that were unsuccessful until I convinced myself that marrying a woman would be ideal and would also dissuade my feelings for my fellow men.

My passion for God did not waver despite my challenges, and I was soon fully convinced that I should get married, start a family, and continue serving God. However, when I got married, it was a terrible experience, and the marriage lasted for only three years. I was unfaithful to my beautiful wife because I frequently sneaked out to meet men for sexual relations. Eventually, my wife found out and was not ready to put up with my unfaithfulness; our marriage fell apart.

All throughout my struggle, I heeded familiar Christian morality but could not find the liberty I desired. My struggle intensified when she left because the lifestyle was no longer a secret. Despite what I was going through, deep within me, I knew that I needed to get a permanent solution to my problem.

Gradually, I came to realize that the Lord understood what I was searching for because, one night, I received a clear message in a dream pointing me to a certain famous deliverance ministry in Uganda for help. In this dream, the president handed me a certificate, which included the name of the lead minister of that deliverance ministry.

In response to my dream, I went to seek that gospel minister, and through his teachings and biblical insights, I got to know that deliverance precedes total freedom. I eventually received the freedom I desired after adhering to the biblical principles I was taught.

This book is a roadmap to freedom from all weird sexual lifestyles to a new, godly, peaceful, and revived lifestyle. In the chapters of this book, I share biblical wisdom and life experiences coupled with prayers, which I believe will open up your understanding to what God means when he says, "Let my people go."

My prayer is that the hand of God touches you as you read this book and sets you free. I also pray that God uses you to help others as you share this message. In Jesus's mighty name.

DEDICATION

I really thank the Holy Spirit for enabling me to do this work. Without him it would be impossible. I thank my wife Anne and our kids for allowing me to take off their time and do the work the Lord has entrusted with us. The Delivered to serve Ministry family has done a great job in encouraging me and praying for this work, may God reward you abundantly. My spiritual parents Pastor Tom and Justine Mugerwa am forever indebted to you, thank you for allowing God to use you to deliver my soul from destruction. All my fellow servants in the vineyard of the Lord, may God bless you for all contributions availed for this book. I dedicate this book to all people of God who desire to see the kingdom of God come in humanity through his deliverance power in Jesus Christ our Lord.

1

Knowledge

Gaining knowledge is essential in all areas where you anticipate victory. The enemy's greatest fear is to be exposed, that is why the intelligence department of any army is their core strength. You cannot attempt to fight an enemy you don't know; knowledge of their strength, number of troops, weaponry, and battle tactics are important. Luke 14:31 says, *"Or what king, going to make war against another king, sits not down first, and consults whether he be able with ten thousand to meet him that cometh against him with twenty thousand?"* All freedom is a result of a battle; it takes a war to receive liberty.

I fought sexual perversion in multiple ways, which included fasting, confessing my sin, reading my Bible, getting married, and praying earnestly. However, none of them worked because there were hidden conundrums about this lifestyle I was not aware of. In addition, my mind was also twisted by my deceptive beliefs.

Lack of knowledge (ignorance or deception) will lead us into captivity or bondage.

I reflected daily on these deceptive beliefs until I met the deliverance minister who, through the scriptures, showed me how I was deceived by my illusive mind.

Isaiah 5:13–14 says, *"Therefore, my people are gone into captivity, because they have no knowledge: and their honorable men are famished, and their multitude dried up with thirst. Therefore, hell hath enlarged herself, and opened her mouth without measure: and their glory, and their multitude, and their pomp, and he that rejoices, shall descend into it."*

Proverbs 24:5–6 says, *"A wise man is strong; yea, a man of knowledge increases strength. For by wise counsel thou shall make thy war: and in multitude of counselors there is safety."* The word of God gives your spirit the right knowledge to fight every spiritual battle wisely.

Psalm 119:24 says, *"Thy testimonies also are my delight and my counselors."* This means that the word of God makes us happy, protects and guides us.

Proverbs 11:9 says, *"An hypocrite with his mouth destroys his neighbor: but through knowledge shall the just be delivered."* This teaches us that knowledge of the word of God will deliver a genuine person.

The deceptive beliefs in contrast with the truth of the word of God included the following:

A. That I was born a homosexual and, therefore, could not change who I was, but John 3:3 and 7 says, *"Jesus answered and said unto him, Verily, verily, I say unto thee, Except a man be born again, he cannot see the kingdom of God. Marvel not that I said unto thee, Ye must be born again."* This means that everyone is born in their own sinful way, but God requires everyone to be born again, that is, to allow Jesus to wash away by his blood that sinful nature which you were born with and give you the nature of God by his Holy Spirit.

B. That it was a normal feeling to desire sleeping with fellow men, but Romans 1:27 says, *"And likewise also the men, leaving the natural use of the woman, burned in their lust one toward another; men with men working that which is unseemly, and receiving in themselves that recompense of their error which was meet."* It means this feeling is a product of lust, working unseemly, and it's an error.

C. Believed that I could go to heaven by the grace of God even if I was gay, but 1 Corinthians 6:9 says, *"Or do you not know that the unrighteous will not inherit the kingdom of God?" Do not be deceived. Neither the sexually immoral, nor idolaters, nor adulterers, nor men who practice homosexuality, nor thieves, nor the greedy, nor drunkards, nor revilers, nor swindlers will inherit the kingdom of God.*

D. I believed that God would just ignore this practice due to my faithfulness in church service, but Psalm 50:16–18 says, *"But unto the wicked God says, What hast thou to do to declare my statutes, or that thou should take my covenant in thy mouth? Seeing thou hates instruction, and casts my words behind thee. When thou saw a thief, then thou consented with him, and hast been partaker with adulterers."*

Also, Matthew 7:22–23 says, *"Many will say to me in that day, Lord, Lord, have we not prophesied in thy name? and in thy name have cast out devils? and in thy name done many wonderful works? And then will I profess unto them, I never knew you: depart from me, ye that work iniquity."*

E. I believed that God knew my heart that I was trying my best though I couldn't help myself, but Zechariah 4:6 says, *"Then he answered and spoke unto me, saying, This is the word of the LORD unto Zerubbabel, saying, Not by might, nor by power, but by my spirit, says the LORD of hosts."* This means that God wants us to ask him for his spirit to help us do what is required of us.

F. I believed that trusting Jesus Christ for my salvation and what He did at the cross for me settles everything, and it doesn't matter what I do with my body; but Revelation 2:23 says, *"And I will kill her children with death; and all the churches shall know that I am he which searches the reins and hearts: and I will give unto every one of you according to your works."* This means continuing with this lifestyle either in heart or in body will bring eternal death.

G. I believed that God was against having multiple partners but faithfulness or marriage to one partner was acceptable, but Leviticus 20:13 says, *"If a man also lie with mankind, as he lies with a woman, both of them have committed an abomination: they shall surely be put to death; their blood shall be upon them."*

H. I believed that other modes of sex with my fellow men, excluding sexual intercourse, was not considered homosexuality, but Matthew 5:28 says, *"But I say unto you, That whosoever looks on a woman (or man) to lust after her (or him) hath committed adultery with her (or him) already in his heart."* This means it's not just about what you do or don't do sexually, it's also about what is playing in your heart.

I. I believed that waiting to confess my sin on my death bed it would guarantee forgiveness; but Isaiah 29:13 says, *"Wherefore the Lord said, Forasmuch as this people draw near me with their mouth, and with their lips do honor me, but have removed their heart far from me, and their fear toward me is taught by the precept of men: Therefore, behold, I will proceed to do a marvelous work among this people, even a marvelous work and a wonder: for the wisdom of their wise men shall perish, and the understanding of their prudent men shall be hid."* This means a mere confession without conversion of the heart will not bring forgiveness.

J. I believed that there were so many of us practicing homosexuality and a loving God wouldn't send us all to hell, but Jude 1:5 and 7 says, *"I will therefore put you in remembrance, though ye once knew this, how that the Lord, having saved the people out of the land of Egypt, afterward destroyed them that believed not. Even as Sodom and Gomorrah, and the cities about them in like manner, giving themselves over to fornication, and going after strange flesh, are set forth for an example, suffering the vengeance of eternal fire."*

Matthew 7:13–14 says, *"Enter you in at the strait gate: for wide is the gate, and broad is the way, that leads to destruction, and many there be which go in there at: Because strait is the gate, and narrow is the way, which leads unto life, and few there be that find it."*

K. I also believed that since many anointed men and women of God are involved in this lifestyle, then God would not criticize it, but 2 Corinthians 11:13–15 says, *"For such are false apostles, deceitful workers, transforming themselves into the apostles of Christ. And no marvel; for Satan himself is transformed into an angel of light. Therefore it is no great thing if his ministers also be transformed as the ministers of righteousness; whose end shall be according to their works."*

L. I also believed that God would have withdrawn his anointing and gifts from me if he had a problem with my lifestyle as I ministered, but Romans 11:29 says, *"For the gifts and calling of God are without repentance."* This shows that our sin may not cause God to withdraw his gifts and anointing because the gifts are for his people who trust in him and not for our personal benefit.

M. I believed that answered prayer was evidence that there was no conflict between me and God, but Ecclesiastes 8:11 says, *"Because sentence against an evil work is not executed speedily, therefore the heart of the sons of men is fully set in them to do evil."*

N. I thought that mutual agreement between me and my partner to do as we please without forcing them meant that I have not hurt them nor hurt God, but Psalm 50:18 and 21 says, *"When thou saw a thief, then thou consented with him, and hast been partaker with adulterers. These things hast thou done, and I kept silence; thou thought that I was altogether such an one as thyself: but I will reprove thee, and set them in order before your eyes."*

O. I believed that loving God and loving my neighbors as I loved myself by sharing my body to meet their sexual needs fulfils the two greatest commandments, but 1 John 5:3 says, *"For this is the love of God, that we keep his commandments: and his commandments are not grievous."* The commandment of God refuses us giving our bodies to sexual perversion.

P. I believed that what I did with my body did not affect my spirit in any way because flesh and blood do not inherit the kingdom of God, so my spirit would remain sanctified even though my body was defiled, but 1 Corinthians 6:20 says, *"For ye are bought with a price: therefore glorify God in your body, and in your spirit, which are God's."*

Q. I thought that supporting this lifestyle financially, celebrating it or being a LGBT activist is advocating for love, but Romans 1:32 says, *"Who knowing the judgment of God, that they which commit such things are worthy of death, not only do the same, but have pleasure in them that do them."* And 2 Chronicles 19:2 says, *"And Jehu the son of Hanani the seer went out to meet him, and said to King Jehoshaphat, Should thou help the ungodly, and love them that hate the LORD? Therefore is wrath upon thee from before the LORD."* This means that he who does perverseness and they that support the perverseness in any way get the same reward, which is the wrath of God.

R. I thought that the scriptures against my lifestyle were outdated or misinterpreted and perhaps not applicable to all, but 2 Peter 3:14–16 says, *"Wherefore, beloved, seeing that ye look for such things, be diligent that ye may be found of him in peace, without spot, and blameless. And account that the long suffering of our Lord is salvation; even as our beloved brother Paul also according to the wisdom given unto him hath written unto you; As also in all his epistles, speaking in them of these things; in which are some things hard to be understood, which they that are unlearned and unstable wrest, as they do also the other scriptures, unto their own destruction."*

This means that many unlearned persons have used the Pauline scriptures to suit their perversions, but it will just produce destruction.

S. I thought that if my financial income and popularity are rooted in my lifestyle, then that's my job, but 2 Corinthians 6:17–18 says, *"Wherefore come out from among them, and be ye separate, says the Lord, and touch not the unclean thing; and I will receive you, And will be a Father unto you, and ye shall be my sons and daughters, says the Lord Almighty."* This means that if you give up on jobs which involve sexual perversions and popularity and turn to God, then He will take care of you as a father does to his children.

T. I thought that Jesus came to give me liberty to enjoy all things and not to be burdened by sexual limitations, but Matthew 11:28–30 says, *"Come unto me, all ye that labor and are heavy laden, and I will give you rest. Take my yoke upon you, and learn of me; for I am meek and lowly in heart: and ye shall find rest unto your souls. For my yoke is easy, and my burden is light."* This means that following Jesus Christ will put a light burden of restrictions on us, but they will produce rest.

U. I thought that knowing about God and believing in Jesus Christ are the only things I needed to please God. I didn't have to perform any works, but Titus 1:16 says, *"They profess that they know God; but in works they deny him, being abominable, and disobedient, and unto every good work reprobate."* This means our works can manifest what we really are on the inside.

V. I thought that my financial support to the poor, the underprivileged and to the work of God would cause God to overlook my lifestyle and sympathize with me, but Revelation 2:19–20 says, *"I know thy works, and charity, and service, and faith, and thy patience, and thy works; and the last to be more than the first. Notwithstanding I have a few things against thee, because thou suffers that woman Jezebel, which calls herself a prophetess, to teach and to seduce my servants to commit fornication, and to eat things sacrificed unto idols."* This means that God wants good works, but purity in the heart has to come first before the works.

W. I also believed that as a born-again Christian, my name is already written in the lamb's book of life and can not be blotted out. Once saved, forever saved. But Exodus 32:33 says, *"And the LORD said unto Moses, Whosoever hath sinned against me, him will I blot out of my book."* And Revelation 3:5 says, *"He that overcomes, the same shall be clothed in white raiment; and I will not blot out his name out of the book of life, but I will confess his name before my Father, and before his angels."*

X. I believed that King David was a man after God's heart, yet he loved Jonathan with a love greater than that of women. This kind of love must be sexual, but Acts 13:36 says, *"For David, after he had served his own generation by the will of God, fell on sleep, and was laid unto his fathers, and saw corruption."* This means David served according to the will of God. Homosexuality is not in the will of God, which concludes that David's relationship with Jonathan was not sexual.

Y. I believed that Jesus was a homosexual because he had a disciple he loved who slept on his bosom, but John 21:20,21, and 24 says, *"Then Peter, turning about, sees the disciple whom Jesus loved following; which also leaned on his breast at supper, and said, Lord, which is he that betrays thee? Peter seeing him says to Jesus, Lord, and what shall this man do? This is the disciple which testifies of these things, and wrote these things: and we know that his testimony is true."* This means that the disciple leaned on Jesus's breast once at the Last Supper in the presence of all, and this love was parental with the purpose of furnishing him with the true testimony of the love of God in the scriptures he was going to write.

Z. I believed that Jesus never spoke against homosexuality; therefore, he condones it, but Luke 17:28–30 says, *"Likewise also as it was in the days of Lot; they did eat, they drank, they bought, they sold, they planted, they built; But the same day that Lot went out of Sodom it rained fire and brimstone from heaven, and destroyed them all. Even thus shall it be in the day when the Son of man is revealed."* This means that the same judgment that happened to Sodom will happen again when Jesus is revealed.

In order for God to help us receive our deliverance, we need to acquire his mindset through scripture. Psalm 81:11–14 says, *"But my people would not hearken to my voice; and Israel would none of me. So I gave them up unto their own hearts' lust: and they walked in their own counsels. Oh that my people had hearkened unto me, and Israel had walked in my ways! I should soon have subdued their enemies and turned my hand against their adversaries."* This means God desires to deliver us from bondage if only we heed his ways, but our refusal means that he will leave us to walk our own lustful ways and heed our own counsel.

Prayer

Father, in the name of Jesus, I repent for all the ignorance and deception that have kept me in bondage. Lord, wash it away from my heart and mind with the blood of Jesus. I ask you to open up my mind that I may understand the truth of your word and give me a heart to know you so that I may walk in your ways. In Jesus's mighty name. Amen.

2

Vision of Heaven

I came to realize that the spirit of sexual perversion usually attacks people with true passion and are committed to please God in all their ways. Such people are usually faithful and are committed to serve their creator with a sincere heart.

I was a committed minister in the church, willing to do anything my fellow ministers regarded as uncomfortable due to their status. I faithfully served the Lord under my leaders, and this opened many great doors for me in the ministry. Everyone was proud of me, and I thought God was also well pleased with me. I also thought of myself as a candidate for heaven though I was struggling with homosexuality.

My physical strength attained through regular workouts was no match in overcoming this spirit if it were a physical battle, but unfortunately, it required spiritual war. And for this reason, my gym membership could not help.

The Levite in scripture had a vision of going to the house of God before he was attacked by this spirit. It is the spirit's strategy to attack people with a heavenly vision. Judges 19:16–18 says, *"And, behold, there came an old man from his work out of the field at even, which was also of mount Ephraim; and he sojourned in Gibeah: but the men of the place were Benjamites. And when he had lifted up his eyes, he saw a wayfaring man in the street of the city: and the old man said, where are you going? and where are you coming from? And he said unto him, We are passing from Bethlehem Judah toward the side of mount Ephraim; from thence am I: and I went to Bethlehem Judah, but I am now going to the house of the LORD; and there is no man that receives me to house."*

This scripture illustrates the cry within the hearts of the many who have been attacked by this spirit of sexual perversion. Their struggles go unnoticed as they endeavor to please the Lord. The Levite wanted to go to God's house, but there was no one to help him realize his vision.

I often professed that I am gay and happy to shut out those who portrayed themselves as perfect (homophobic). However, deep within me, I was crying for help. This is the reason why victims of sexual perversion are creating their own churches, schools, businesses, adoptions, grants, etc.

Physical expressions, including smiles, body structures, fancy outfits, and participations in gay pride parades are a façade to the deep emotions of those suppressed by this spirit. This creates an opportunity for the spirit to intensify its deceptions within the victim's mind. The spirit works tirelessly to connect you to people who may appear as caring counselors but have a hidden agenda to quench your "heavenly vision."

After I was delivered from the control of this spirit, I repented to God and also shared my story. However, I faced such discrimination from the church people who never understood my heavenly vision. The reason I repented and shared my story was in obedience to the word of the Lord. Proverbs 28:13 says, *"He that covers his sins shall not prosper: but whoso confesses and forsakes them shall have mercy."* But instead of receiving moral support and encouragement to help me pursue my heavenly vision, my purported church friends turned away.

I became so lonely, and this spirit came back and fed me more lies. I also started doubting whether what I had done was in God's will since I had not received the support I anticipated from the church.

But I give thanks to God because He had a plan for me. God visited and spoke to a friend of mine in a dream. Ironically, this friend had determined never to speak to me again after hearing my story. God spoke to her about my honesty and asked her to fully support me in everything that I needed. The Lord further explained to her that I was his chosen vessel to witness for him in all nations around the world.

My circumstances were similar to what happened to Paul the apostle after he repented and pledged to serve the Lord. The church was blind and did not embrace him but continued to condemn him for his old lifestyle. It was until God visited one member of the church and told him the truth about Paul's changed heart. Paul was praying for help. Acts 9:11–15 says, *"And the Lord said unto him, arise, and go into the street which is called Straight, and enquire in the house of Judas for one called Saul, of Tarsus: for, behold, he prays [in his heart], And hath seen in a vision a man named Ananias coming in, and putting his hand on him, that he might receive his sight. Then Ananias answered, Lord, I have heard by many of this man, how much evil he hath done to thy saints at Jerusalem: And here he hath authority from the chief priests to bind all that call on thy name. But the Lord said unto him, Go thy way: for he is a chosen vessel unto me, to bear my name before the Gentiles, and kings, and the children of Israel."*

Ananias tried to remind the Lord of Paul's wickedness, but God had heard his heart's cry and insisted that Ananias should go to Paul because he was now a chosen servant of God.

We thank God that Ananias obeyed and supported Paul to realize his heavenly vision. Judas Iscariot is another disciple of Jesus Christ who the church lost because no one helped him realize his heavenly vision. After Judas realized his sin, he repented and returned the money he had received as a bribe. However, due to lack of support and with nobody accepting him back, Judas was deceived to the point of committing suicide. Matthew 27:3–5 says, *"Then Judas, which had betrayed him, when he saw that he was condemned, repented himself, and brought again the thirty pieces of silver to the chief priests and elders, Saying, I have sinned in that I have betrayed the innocent blood. And they said, What is that to us? see thou to that.*

And he cast down the pieces of silver in the temple, and departed, and went and hanged himself."

Many individuals controlled by this spirit of sexual perversion have committed suicide because there is no one to answer their inner cry for help.

For this reason, I suggest not believing in their words and actions but believing in their heart. I have come to realize that a person can have a good heart while their mind and body are controlled by evil forces. This usually causes people to speak and act contrary to their heart. Isaiah 11:3 says, *"And shall make him of quick understanding in the fear of the LORD: and he shall not judge after the sight of his eyes, neither reprove after the hearing of his ears."*

There is an urgent call for compassion in the church because God will not anoint you to deliver a person you don't have compassion for. Jesus's first response to anyone who came to him was compassion before the power to heal them manifested. Matthew 14:14 says, *"And Jesus went forth, and saw a great multitude, and was moved with compassion toward them, and he healed their sick."* When Jesus looked at the multitudes and realized what was in their heart, which caused them to come seeking for him, he had compassion for them and then met their real need for healing. Matthew 9:36–37 says, *"But when he saw the multitudes, he was moved with compassion on them, because they fainted, and were scattered abroad, as sheep having no shepherd. Then says he unto his disciples, the harvest truly is plenteous, but the laborers are few; Pray you therefore the Lord of the harvest, that he will send forth laborers into his harvest."*

There are many people who need help, but God has few laborers who are compassionate and willing to be part of the healing process. It is essential that the church prays for the fruit of the Holy Spirit called "compassion," and whoever receives it also receives power to set the captives of this spirit free. Judges 21:13–14 says, *"And the whole congregation sent some to speak to the children of Benjamin that were in the rock Rimmon, and to call peaceably unto them. And Benjamin came again at that time; and they gave them wives which they had saved alive of the women of Jabeshgilead."*

The children of Israel had compassion on the victims of the spirit of sexual perversion who had become homosexuals. They accepted their repentance and allowed them to return to the congregation. They also gave them wives to marry according to God's law of nature.

To those who currently are, or have, previously been victims of sexual perversion, I pray that you will be humble enough and ask for help from the right people. I also pray that God gives you grace to endure the pain before your help arrives because it shall surely come, and a greater part of it is in this book. 2 Timothy 2:10–12 says, *"Therefore I endure all things for the elect's sakes, that they may also obtain the salvation which is in Christ Jesus with eternal glory. It is a faithful saying: For if we be dead with him, we shall also live with him: If we suffer, we shall also reign with him: if we deny him, he also will deny us."*

Prayer

Father, in the name of Jesus, I am sorry for not being able to see what you see in the lives of people. I repent for speaking and acting proudly against your people. Lord, cleanse my heart of all the fruit of Satan, which include hatred, lust, malice, and judging with the eyes, with the blood of Jesus.

Lord, give me your spirit to enable me hear the cry for help in the heart of any victim of sexual perversion. Lord, give me the spirit of meekness to open up myself for help and to also ask for it.

Lord, give me an enduring heart so that I may be able to seek, stand, and walk with you and never deny you. In Jesus's name. Amen.

3

Defiling Spirit

When an individual or creature is possessed by the spirit, which causes sexual perversion, the two become one. This oneness makes the spirit take full control of your spirit, soul, and body. A defiled human spirit acquires the character of the evil spirit and manifests in your dreams, thoughts, senses, and actions. It is only a spirit that can control a soul and a body; for this reason, man can either be controlled by an evil spirit or by the Holy Spirit of God. Whichever is in control will determine the preferred choices in your life.

Animals can also be controlled by a spirit because they have a soul. Please note that "emotions/feelings" are part of the soul. The difference between an animal and man is that animals only have a soul and body, but man has the human spirit, soul, and body. In human beings, the spirit is supposed to be in charge of the soul and body. However, because of sin, the human spirit lost its God-given authority and now can be subdued by the spirit of Satan.

In scripture, we see the spirit of God possessing an animal and caused it to speak. Numbers 22:28–30 says, *"And the LORD opened the mouth of the ass, and she said unto Balaam, What have I done unto thee, that thou hast smitten me these three times? And Balaam said unto the ass, because thou hast mocked me: I would there were a sword in mine hand, for now would I kill thee. And the ass said unto Balaam, Am not I thine ass, upon which thou hast ridden ever since I was thine unto this day? Was I ever wont to do so unto thee? And he said, No."*

Scripture also shows us when an evil spirit or Satan possessed an animal and caused it to speak. Genesis 3:1–4 says, *"Now the serpent was more subtle than any beast of the field which the LORD God had made. And he said unto the woman, Yea, hath God said, you shall not eat of every tree of the garden? And the woman said unto the serpent, we may eat of the fruit of the trees of the garden: But of the fruit of the tree which is in the midst of the garden, God hath said, you shall not eat of it, neither shall ye touch it, lest ye die. And the serpent said unto the woman, you shall not surely die."*

It is also evident in scripture that the spirit of God can come upon you and cause you to do what you cannot do by yourself. 1 Samuel 19:22–24 says, *"Then went Saul also to Ramah, and came to a great well that is in Sechu: and he asked and said, Where are Samuel and David? And one said, Behold, they are at Naioth in Ramah. And he went thither to Naioth in Ramah: and the Spirit of God was upon him also, and he went on, and prophesied, until he came to Naioth in Ramah. And he stripped off his clothes also, and prophesied before Samuel in like manner, and lay down naked all that day and all that night. Wherefore they say, is Saul also among the prophets?"*

In contrast, when you are possessed by an evil spirit, it will cause you to do things against your will. Mark 5:2–5 says, *"And when Jesus was come out of the ship, immediately there met him out of the tombs a man with an unclean spirit, Who had his dwelling among the tombs; and no man could bind him, no, not with chains. Because that he had been often bound with fetters and chains, and the chains had been plucked asunder by him, and the fetters broken in pieces: neither could any man tame him. And always, night and day, he was in the mountains, and in the tombs, crying, and cutting himself with stones."*

Before my deliverance, the spirit of sexual perversion caused me to lust after my fellow men. My feelings for the opposite sex were defiled with a preference to same-sex intercourse over heterosexual ones. Ephesians 4:17–20 says, *"This I say therefore, and testify in the Lord, that you henceforth walk not as other Gentiles walk, in the vanity of their mind, Having their understanding darkened, being alienated from the life of God through the ignorance that is in them, because of the blindness of their heart: Who being past feeling [defiled feelings] have given themselves over unto lasciviousness [life without restraints], to work all uncleanness with greediness [passion]? But ye have not so learned Christ."*

I reached a point when I desired to sleep with anything and anyone including animals, young kids, chickens, mentally ill people, to satisfy my sexual urge.

This scripture is very clear that when your connection to God is fractured at the spiritual level, you go beyond the point of natural feelings and give yourself to a life of lasciviousness, which drives you to do any kind of uncleanness with passion. I have seen people with a fantasy of eating poop and drinking piss during sexual intercourse.

Today, I am convinced that this kind of lifestyle is not from Christ, nor is it taught by the spirit of God. When I was twelve years old, I was molested by a nanny. That encounter greatly affected my immediate future. I came to realize this because whenever I went to church, I would sometimes feel like raping someone, especially young girls and boys. I was deceived in my mind that I would get more pleasure and intimacy from breaking their virginity. I thank God that all this never happened in real life however much as it was playing in my mind.

When I made love to my ex-wife, I mostly wanted to have anal sex, but thank God she never accepted such perversion.

I indulged in watching pornographic movies and reading pornographic articles, and I also had pornographic materials on my cell phone. I masturbated whenever I got a chance in public restrooms, in the bushes where no one was watching, in the lake when we went swimming, and especially in the bathroom whenever I was taking a shower. I also cut out a hole in my mattress for masturbation purposes.

During my first married life, I occasionally left my ex-wife at home and went out to meet young men in secure places like at the beach or at their apartments for sexual encounters. The things I was doing are proof that some evil spirit was controlling my soul and body, which caused me to do things I could never have done in my right mind.

I agree with scripture that I was possessed by the spirit of sexual perversion that defiled my feelings and desires. This spirit is responsible for all kinds of perversions in people's lives as illustrated in scripture. These include pornography, masturbation, incest, rape, oral sex, drunken sex, anal sex, bestiality, pedophilia, coprophilia, voyeurism, fornication, adultery, lesbianism, sodomy, and others. As the scripture in Genesis 19:5–8 says, *"And they called unto Lot, and said unto him, where are the men who came in to thee this night? Bring them out unto us, that we may know them. And Lot went out at the door unto them, and shut the door after him, And said, I pray you, brethren, do not so wickedly. Behold now, I have two daughters which have not known man; let me, I pray you, bring them out unto you, and do ye to them as is good in your eyes: only unto these men do nothing; for therefore came they under the shadow of my roof."*

You can be born already possessed by the spirit of sexual perversion if it was controlling your parents or ancestors as Psalm 51:5 declares, *"Behold, I was sharpen in iniquity; and in sin did my mother conceive me."*

We all come from different corners of the earth and are associated to some kind of sin ever since the fall of man. Sexual perversion is one of the many generational sins that affect man. Romans 3:23 says, *"For all have sinned, and come short of the glory of God."* This affirms the need to be born again and sever the control of sin. After which, you need to welcome the spirit of God to take control of your life and lead you into the kingdom of God.

John 3:3 says, *"Jesus answered and said unto him, Verily, verily, I say unto thee, Except a man be born again, he cannot see the kingdom of God."*

The spirit of lust intends to kill you and make sure that you lose the purpose of God in your life. Lust also comes in various ways, including lust for; sex, food, drugs, power, wealth, fame, alcohol, tobacco, and others.

Numbers 11:33–34 says, *"And while the flesh was yet between their teeth, before it was chewed, the wrath of the LORD was kindled against the people, and the LORD smote the people with a very great plague. And he called the name of that place Kibroth-hattaavah: because there they buried the people that lusted."*

Incest is also caused by the spirit of lust or sexual perversion and will cause you to have sexual desires for your relative. 2 Samuel 13:2 and 14–15 says, *"And Amnon was so vexed, that he fell sick for his sister Tamar; for she was a virgin; and Amnon thought it hard for him to do anything to her. Howbeit he would not hearken unto her voice: but, being stronger than she, forced her, and lay with her. Then Amnon hated her exceedingly; so that the hatred wherewith he hated her was greater than the love wherewith he had loved her. And Amnon said unto her, Arise, be gone."*

The spirit of lust can also influence the way you dress, walk, and talk and your general demeanor. Your behavior will be intentional to attract and seduce people into desiring to be sexually involved with you, but Isaiah 3:16–17 says, *"Moreover the LORD says, Because the daughters of Zion are haughty, and walk with stretched forth necks and wanton eyes, walking and mincing as they go, and making a tinkling with their feet: Therefore the Lord will smite with a scab the crown of the head of the daughters of Zion, and the LORD will discover their secret parts."* The spirit of sexual perversion can cause a person to use drugs or alcohol to intoxicate a person they want to have intercourse with.

Genesis 19:31–32 says, *"And the firstborn said unto the younger, our father is old, and there is not a man in the earth to come in unto us after the manner of all the earth: Come, let us make our father drink wine, and we will lie with him, that we may preserve seed of our father. And they made their father drink wine that night: and the firstborn went in, and lay with her father; and he perceived not when she lay down, nor when she arose."*

The scriptures continue to warn us in Habakkuk 2:15–16 saying, *"Woe unto him that gives his neighbor drink, that puts thy bottle to him, and makes him drunken also, that thou may look on their nakedness! Thou art filled with shame for glory: drink thou also, and let thy foreskin be uncovered: the cup of the LORD's right hand shall be turned unto thee, and shameful spewing shall be on thy glory."*

All sexual activities against nature are caused by the spirit of sexual perversion. Romans 1:26–27 says, *"For this cause God gave them up unto vile affections: for even their women did change the natural use into that which is against nature. And likewise also the men, leaving the natural use of the woman, burned in their lust one toward another; men with men working that which is unseemly, and receiving in themselves that recompense of their error which was meet."*

Prayer

Father, in Jesus's name, I repent opening a door to the defiling spirit. Lord, cleanse me with the blood of Jesus of all the defilement whether I was born with it or acquired it in the course of my life. I give you authority to purge my spirit, soul, and body of all spirits of defilement with the blood of Jesus and fill me with your Holy Spirit that I may serve the living God with a godly lifestyle. In Jesus's name. Amen.

4

The Power of Lust

Sexual perversion has the ability to subdue all our five senses and render the victim powerless. In scripture, perversion is compared to a drunken person who loses their control on hearing, touching, smelling, seeing, and tasting. Revelation 17:1–2 says, *"And there came one of the seven angels which had the seven vials, and talked with me, saying unto me, Come here; I will show unto thee the judgment of the great whore that sits upon many waters: With whom the kings of the earth have committed fornication, and the inhabitants of the earth have been made drunk with the wine of her fornication."*

I recall an incident when a bush was the preferred place to get involved with someone, yet there was nothing more than rocks and broken tree branches. The roughness in the area caused bleeding, but neither of us cared about the pain nor the bleeding until we were done. This is an indication that none of us were in control of our own senses at all. Some of the things we did were very nasty and unclean, but our perception was meagre. Our taste was polluted, for we did not care about what we ate, and our sense of smell was impaired such that the smell of excretions did not matter to us.

This indicates that the person loses their basic reasoning or understanding of the human mind when the spirit of lust has total control over them. Proverbs 6:32–33 says, *"But whosoever commits adultery with a woman/man lacks understanding: he/she that does it destroys his/her own soul. A wound and dishonor shall he/she get; and his/her reproach shall not be wiped away."*

There was no solace for my soul after every sexual encounter. I always felt worthless, restless, and never satisfied, like a person chasing after the wind. No guy was satisfying enough no matter how good they looked physically, emotionally, socially, and financially. Isaiah 57:20–21 says, *"But the wicked are like the troubled sea, when it cannot rest, whose waters cast up mire and dirt. There is no peace, says my God, to the wicked."*

There are many things we do in life that are praiseworthy before men yet are considered wicked in God's sight. Such things will never give us satisfaction or rest. My ordeals caused me to start doubting God's existence because I could not find help, peace, joy, and the true meaning of life. Job 35:10–13 says, *"But none saith, Where is God my maker, who gives songs in the night; Who teaches us more than the beasts of the earth, and makes us wiser than the fowls of heaven? There they cry, but none gives answer, because of the pride of evil men. Surely God will not hear vanity, neither will the Almighty regard it."*

My doubts about the existence of God created suicidal thoughts inside me. Psalm 14:1 says, *"The fool has said in his heart, there is no God. They are corrupt, they have done abominable works, and there is none that does good."* Whenever our mind is tarnished and we are doing detestable works, thoughts doubting the existence of God will develop within us.

The Lord Jesus spoke about these controlling spirits as very strong. He also told us that when we welcome His spirit into our lives, He is more powerful and will deliver us from their control. Luke 11:21–22 says, *"When a strong man armed keeps his palace, his goods are in peace: But when a stronger than he shall come upon him, and overcome him, he takes from him all his armor wherein he trusted, and divides his spoils."*

Never give up on your life irrespective of whatever the situation. There is always help if you can tarry a little longer. Suicide is never a solution but an admittance of failure for eternity. Ezekiel 22:14 says,

"Can your heart endure, or can your hands be strong, in the days that I shall deal with thee? I the LORD has spoken it, and will do it."

The man who was controlled by a legion of evil spirits had major problems. His body was covered in bleeding wounds; he slept in the tombs, was naked, and had no friends. He was also forsaken by his family because they didn't have a solution to his problem. But because he endured, one day, the Lord headed his way with a solution.

When I was about to give up on my life, the Lord sent Chris[guy who gave directions to the deliverance church] to me, and he came with a solution. Right now, I believe the Lord has sent this book to you with a solution. Mark 5:1–6 says, *"And they came over unto the other side of the sea, into the country of the Gadarenes. And when he was come out of the ship, immediately there met him out of the tombs a man with an unclean spirit, Who had his dwelling among the tombs; and no man could bind him, no, not with chains: Because that he had been often bound with fetters and chains, and the chains had been plucked asunder by him, and the fetters broken in pieces: neither could any man tame him. And always, night and day, he was in the mountains, and in the tombs, crying, and cutting himself with stones. But when he saw Jesus afar off, he ran and worshipped him."*

This man never committed suicide even though he was as good as dead as he slept with the dead in the cemetery. You are a human spirit, and you live in a body. This means that you will never cease to exist because spirits don't die. Suicide is a continuation of your suffering but in a different world. Luke 16:22–25 says, *"And it came to pass, that the beggar died, and was carried by the angels into Abraham's bosom: the rich man also died and was buried; and in hell he lift up his eyes, being in torments, and sees Abraham afar off, and Lazarus in his bosom. And he cried and said, Father Abraham, have mercy on me, and send Lazarus, that he may dip the tip of his finger in water, and cool my tongue; for I am tormented in this flame. But Abraham said, Son, remember that thou in thy lifetime received thy good things, and likewise Lazarus evil things: but now he is comforted, and thou art tormented."*

The rich man was still existing and feeling the pain of the fire even after death but in the world of spirits; therefore, you don't want to have such an experience forever.

Prayer

Father, in the name of Jesus, I repent of all drunkenness that I have acquired through the spirit of sexual perversion. Wash it out of my life and senses with the blood of Jesus. Lord, I ask you to forgive me for all the abominable acts that I have done before you. Restore my true understanding and senses with your Holy Spirit.

Deliver me, Lord, from the power of sexual perversion and its suicidal thoughts with the blood of Jesus. Give me peace in my heart that I may have your rest. In Jesus's name. Amen.

5

My Excitement

The spirit of sexual perversion is mainly rooted in things that excite people. Excitement is one of the main channels through which Satan enters our lives. In moments of excitement, the victim is unaware of the consequences of their actions. My first sexual encounter was with the guy who I met at the cyber café after watching gay porn, which excited me because I had never seen such a thing in my life. He became my friend, and later, I invited him at my house where we watched a gay porn movie. After the movie, we joked about some scenes, and I told him that "these men are crazy" and was wondering how they could do such a dirty thing, oblivious that as I watched and laughed, I was also being initiated into it.

The spirit of perversion is always present where there is excitement, looking for an opportunity to devour someone. Judges 19:22 says, *"Now as they were making their hearts merry, behold, the men of the city, certain sons of Belial, beset the house round about, and beat at the door, and spoke to the master of the house, the old man, saying, Bring forth the man that came into your house, that we may know [have a sexual affair with] him."* Here, this spirit used the atmosphere of excitement caused by food and drinking. It will always set its traps and agents where you get excited. It may be at gyms, basketball games, vacation spots, education trips, music festivals, birthday parties, movie theaters, political rallies, get-togethers, sports bars, dance clubs, religious events, work places, walking trails, hair salons, massage parlors, beauty pageant events, gambling sites, drug dealing stations, and many others. The spirit of sexual perversion always took advantage of my swimming hobby to set me up with guys at the beach before my time of deliverance.

A sense of excitement aroused within me whenever I saw someone with a seductive body at the beach. Its agents usually have a convincing tongue and builds trust from the prospective victim who is unaware of its advances. Proverbs 5:3–6 says, *"For the lips of a strange woman [spirit of sexual perversion] drop as a honeycomb, and her mouth is smoother than oil: But her end is bitter as wormwood, sharp as a two-edged sword. Her feet go down to death; her steps take hold on hell. Lest you should ponder the path of life, her ways are moveable, that you cannot know them."*

The spirit (strange woman) uses a soft and persuasive tongue with words like "Try it. If you do not like it, you can quit." Unfortunately, the victim is unaware of the consequences of their choices from that day onward. In reality, however, the continuous excitements only make it harder for them to quit. Mark 8:35–38 says, *"For whosoever will save his life [excitement] shall lose it; but whosoever shall lose his life [excitement] for my sake and the gospel's, the same shall save it. For what shall it profit a man, if he shall gain the whole world, and lose his own soul? Or what shall a man give in exchange for his soul? Whosoever therefore shall be ashamed of me and of my words in this adulterous and sinful generation; of him also shall the Son of man be ashamed, when he cometh in the glory of his Father with the holy angels."*

You can be delivered by the blood of Jesus when you forsake the excitements of life offered by this spirit and choose Jesus to take control of your life. Philippians 3:8 says, *"Yes doubtless, and I count all things but loss for the Excellency of the knowledge of Christ Jesus my Lord: for whom I have suffered the loss of all things, and do count them but dung, that I may win Christ."*

Engaging in any form of sexual perversion forms a covenant (soul-tie) between you and the symbolic spirit of the other person.

Exodus 23:32–33 says, *"You shall make no covenant with them, nor with their gods (spirit of sexual perversion). They shall not dwell in thy land (body), lest they make you to sin against me: for if you serve their gods, it will surely be a snare unto you."*

It is undoubtedly impossible to rid yourself of this spirit of sexual perversion; it is a snare. It is only Jesus Christ who can deliver you when you give him control over your spirit, mind, and body through the biblical principles we are discussing in this book. John 8:36 says, *"If the Son therefore shall make you free, ye shall be free indeed."*

Various programs have been designed and offered to people as guidelines to freedom from sexual perversion. These programs have failed because sexual perversion is a spiritual bondage that cannot be overcome through physical means but through Jesus Christ [spiritual power] who can bring about this transformation.

Prayer

Father, in the name of Jesus, I repent of all excitements that have blinded me and caused me to fall into the snares of the spirit of sexual perversion. Lord, wash away the spirit of excitement from my senses with the blood of Jesus. Give me your spirit of meekness and truth to guide me toward my freedom. In Jesus's name. Amen.

6

Is This a Family Thing?

As I mentioned earlier, after I received my freedom from the spirit of lust, I shared my story at church. My testimony was recorded and later broadcast on national radio and television. Among the many who listened and watched on television was my younger half-brother.

I was shocked when he came to me and shared his struggle with homosexuality, yet he also was a professed Christian. He told me that he was one of the first porn stars in the country, and they recorded their gay porn movies from a neighboring country because it was illegal to do such activities in our own country. With tears in his eyes, he told me that he had contracted the HIV-AIDS virus.

I was so sorry to hear that, but I realized that I was not the only one in the family dealing with this spirit of sexual perversion; it was deeply rooted within our family. Our case may not be similar to yours, but it may be true for many after thorough research.

People are usually initiated into sexual perversion by close relatives through seduction, molestation, rape, or through demonic family covenants. A close family member living a perverted sexual lifestyle gives the spirit of lust access into the family, thereby creating a spiritual covenant for all family members.

The truth I understood from scripture and through experience led me to an extensive inquiry about my parents. I discovered that my father married a woman from his own clan, which is a form of incest.

I mentioned earlier that incest is a form of sexual perversion caused by the spirit of lust. It was also ironic that I belonged to the same clan with the young man I was first involved with. This confirmed that this was not a coincidence but a preplanned process beyond my control.

The Bible illustrates that King David had a similar challenge. 2 Samuel 12:11–12 says, *"Thus says the LORD, Behold, I will raise up evil against you out of your own house, and I will take your wives before your eyes, and give them unto your neighbor [family member], and he shall lie with your wives in the sight of this sun. For you did it secretly: but I will do this thing before all Israel [publicly], and before the sun."*

God spoke to his servant, David, about the consequences of sexual perversion, that a time would come when the spirit of lust will be exposed. King David's children manifested different sexual perversions due to the same spirit he had given access into his family.

A time came when David's secret (sexual perversion by sleeping with other people's wives) was exposed by the spirit of lust because it had access into his family.

King David's son, King Solomon, in 1 Kings 11:1–3 says, *"But King Solomon loved many strange women, together with the daughter of Pharaoh, women of the Moabites, Ammonites, Edomites, Zidonians, and Hittites; of the nations concerning which the LORD said unto the children of Israel, Ye shall not have sexual affairs with them, neither shall they have sexual affairs with you: for surely they will turn away your heart after their gods (family spirits): Solomon clave unto these in love."*

King David's son, Amnon, and daughter, Tamar, in 2 Samuel 13:10–11 says, *"And Amnon said unto Tamar, Bring the meat into the chamber, that I may eat of thine hand. And Tamar took the cakes which she had made, and brought them into the chamber to Amnon her brother. And when she had brought them unto him to eat, he took hold of her, and said unto her, Come lie with me, my sister. And she answered him, Nay, my brother, do not force me; for no such thing ought to be done in Israel: do not thou this folly. Howbeit he would not hearken unto her voice: but, being stronger than she, forced her, and lay with her."*

Tamar denounced his brother's advances as foolishness, but Amnon was stronger and overpowered her. Innate sin is so strong for your mind to resist and can only be overcome by a greater power, which is the blood of Jesus, coupled with repentance for total deliverance.

King David's son, Absalom, in 2 Samuel 16:21–22 says, *"And Ahithophel said unto Absalom, Go in unto thy father's concubines, which he hath left to keep the house; and all Israel shall hear that thou art abhorred of thy father: then shall the hands of all that are with thee be strong. So they spread Absalom a tent upon the top of the house; and Absalom went in [had sexual affairs] unto his father's concubines in the sight of all Israel."*

King David's children were enticed into sexual perversion by friends, counselors, peers—an action impelled by the spiritual covenant with the spirit of lust. They could not comprehend what was noble from what was morally wrong.

Lamentations 5:7–8 says, *"Our fathers have sinned, and are not [they are dead]; and we have borne [carried on] their iniquities. Servants [evil spirits] have ruled over us. There is none that doth deliver us out of their hand."* This scripture tells of a child's disparaging cry about the ancestor's sins which have brought him significant peril and lack of self-control. It is only by divine intervention that deliverance can manifest in his family.

In contrast, both good and evil dispositions can be passed on from generation to generation. 2 Timothy 1:5 says, *"When I call to remembrance the unfeigned faith that is in thee, which dwelt first in thy grandmother Lois, and thy mother Eunice; and I am persuaded that in thee also."*

Paul was pondering Timothy's genuine faith, which must have come from his mother, Eunice, and his grandmother, Lois.

Family members, under the control of the spirit of sexual perversion, usually have persistent sexual dreams, which are a seal of proof of their spiritual covenant with this spirit. Such dreams often cause one to experience uncontrolled lust throughout the day.

Deuteronomy 23:10–11 says, *"If there be among you any man, that is not clean [defiled)] by reason of uncleanness that chances him by night [sexual dream], then shall he go abroad out of the camp, he shall not come within the camp: But it shall be, when evening comes on, he shall wash [repent] himself with water: and when the sun is down, he shall come into the camp again."*

We understand from this scripture that sexual dreams are not from God; neither are they scientific, but they are spiritual, and they defile a person's spirit and mind. That's why God commands us to repent and denounce those spiritual covenants and be washed clean through the blood of Jesus.

I also recall that if I was not involved with a guy for a couple of days, I would get sexual dreams and wake up with wet undergarments. Consequently, I would lust after every nice-looking guy. This made me feel empty spiritually, like I had lost all my anointing for the ministry.

Sexual dreams are satanic avenues that drain gospel ministers of their anointing before a ministry appointment. This aborts every spiritual pregnancy (a miracle, a breakthrough, or a special blessing) that the Lord was preparing to manifest in someone's life.

Combating Family Spirits

God called Abraham and commanded him to come out of three major "spiritual places" for him to be blessed and for God's promises in his life to come to pass. Genesis 12:1–3 says, *"Now the LORD had said unto Abram, Get you out of thy country, and from thy kindred, and from thy father's house, unto a land that I will show you: And I will make of you a great nation, and I will bless you, and make thy name great; and you shall be a blessing: And I will bless them that bless you, and curse him that curses you: and in you shall all families of the earth be blessed."* For you to be a blessing to others you must have come out of your country, kindred [clan] and from your father's house.

Coming out of "your country" means letting go of your conceptions that are contrary to the word and principles of God. These include lustful thoughts, stealing, envy, unbelief, covetousness, wickedness, deceit, lasciviousness, an evil eye, blasphemy, pride, foolishness, uncleanness, idolatry, witchcraft, hatred, anger, compromise, unforgiveness, fear, worry, sorrow, complaints, drunkenness, and an evil tongue. Psalm 66:18 says, *"If I regard iniquity in my heart, the Lord will not hear me."*

The contents of the heart determine whether God will answer your prayer for deliverance or not. Failure to come out of your country (evil in heart) will deny you true deliverance.

The process of deliverance taught me that homosexuality is likened to a tree: the worldly thoughts (roots) feed the lifestyle (tree). I focused on stopping the homosexual lifestyle without dealing with the worldly thoughts. I believe there are many others who try to cut the tree without removing the roots from the ground, and soon or later the tree sprouts.

Job 14:7–9 says, *"For there is hope of a tree, if it be cut down, that it will sprout again, and that the tender branch thereof will not cease. Though the root thereof wax old in the earth, and the stock thereof die in the ground; Yet through the scent of water it will bud, and bring forth boughs like a plant."*

Whenever I was angry, disappointed, or depressed, I would desire to have sexual encounters to pacify myself. Such seducers are likened to a scent of water that causes the tree to sprout again.

"Your country" may also be contrasted with the spiritual world where your spirit is held in captivity. There is a world of sin (where people who are not born again live spiritually), a world of tradition and ancestral spirits (where Abram lived spiritually), a world of sorcery (where the people of Samaria lived spiritually), a world of religion (where Paul lived spiritually), a world of sickness (where the man at the pool of Bethesda lived spiritually), a world of the dead (where the man with a legion lived spiritually), a world of false prophets/occultism (where the girl who followed Paul and Silas lived spiritually), and many others. God has always been delivering His people from such spiritual worlds. 1 John 5:4–5 says, *"For whatsoever is born of God overcomes the world: and this is the victory that overcomes the world, even our faith. Who is he that overcomes the world, but he that believeth that Jesus is the Son of God?"* Overcoming these spiritual worlds begins with you accepting Jesus Christ as your Lord and personal savior.

Our given names are a means by which family spirits identify those who belong to them. God took the initial step in Abram's deliverance by giving him a new name, Abraham.

Genesis 17:5 says, *"Neither shall your name any more be called Abram, but your name shall be Abraham; for a father of many nations have I made thee."*

My activities on social media induced me to set up multiple accounts under different names to suit the purposes of the accounts. I was unaware that the spirit of lust was giving me various names according to the work it was using me for on the different social media platforms. This is what this spirit does with anyone it controls.

There is a great battle within the spiritual world, including Christian circles, when it comes to naming a newly born child. Family spirits usually introduce a name to the parents' minds with the purpose of monitoring this child through this name. It may also be the same name of one of the parents such that whatever has been happening in the life of the parent may also be passed on to the child's life. This is exactly what happened at the birth of John the Baptist. Luke 1:59–63 says, *"And it came to pass, that on the eighth day they came to circumcise the child; and they called him Zacharias, after the name of his father. And his mother answered and said, Not so; but he shall be called John. And they said unto her, there is none of thy kindred that is called by this name. And they made signs to his father, how he would have him called. And he asked for a writing table, and wrote, saying, His name is John. And they marveled all."*

Due to influence of family spirits and their desire to conform to family norms, the family members wanted to name the child after his father, who was a fruitless minister. Fortunately, Zacharias and his wife had heard from the Lord and both obeyed to give the child the name they received from the angel of the Lord.

Every name has a meaning and a covenant attached to it that foretells the future of the owner. If the meaning of the name is satanic, then there is an evil covenant and a monitoring spirit following the name and the individual to fulfil the destiny desired by the family spirit. 1 Samuel 25:25 says, *"Let not my lord, I pray you, regard this man of Belial, even Nabal: for as his name is, so is he; Nabal is his name, and folly is with him."* Nabal's name means "foolish," and the family spirit of foolishness controlled his life. A given name is very important in the spiritual world. God gave his son, Jesus, a name that is above all names as a reward for the price He paid to redeem humanity.

A God-given name means that it is covenanted and the Holy Spirit follows it to fulfil the destiny desired by God for that person. 1 Chronicles 22:9 says, *"Behold, a son shall be born to you, who shall be a man of rest; and I will give him rest from all his enemies round about: for his name shall be Solomon, and I will give peace and quietness unto Israel in his days."* A God-given name brought peace upon an entire nation such that no one could rise against it in battle.

It is wise to renounce your name or even change it if you consider it to have a satanic meaning. Alternatively, you can repent and denounce the family covenants behind the name. Dedicate the name to God's covenant with the blood of Jesus and cast away all monitoring spirits following the name with the blood of Jesus. In addition, ask God's blessing upon your life like Jabez did.

1 Chronicles 4:9–10 says, *"And Jabez was more honourable than his brethren: and his mother called his name Jabez, saying, Because I bare him with sorrow. And Jabez called on the God of Israel, saying, Oh that you would bless me indeed, and enlarge my coast, and that your hand might be with me, and that you would keep me from evil, that it may not grieve me! And God granted him that which he requested."* Jabez's name was influenced by an evil covenant

which caused him sorrow and deprived him of provision, he had no influence in matters concerning life.

Coming out of your "kindred or clan" means letting go of the traditions that connect us to our ancestors which are contrary to the word and principles of God. These may include our given names, choice of marriage partners, people we associate with, preferred places, and possessions.

1 Peter 1:18–19 says, *"Forasmuch as you know that you were not redeemed with corruptible things, as silver and gold, from your vain conversation received by tradition from your fathers; but with the precious blood of Christ, as of a lamb without blemish and without spot."* We can only come out of our kindred by the blood of Jesus.

Many people, including the servants of God, have suffered and still suffer because of the inability to identify the source of their struggles. Moses was a great man of God who failed to identify the controlling spirit in his clan (tribe), and this spirit ultimately compromised his destiny. Moses was born in the tribe of Levi.

The Levites gave the spirit of anger access, and it destroyed destinies of many from this tribe. Genesis 49:1, 5–7 says, *"And Jacob called unto his sons, and said, Gather yourselves together, that I may tell you that which shall befall you in the last days. Simeon and Levi are brethren; instruments of cruelty are in their habitations. O my soul, come not thou into their secret; unto their assembly, mine honor, be not thou united: for in their anger they slew a man, and in their self-will they dug down a wall. Cursed be their anger, for it was fierce; and their wrath, for it was cruel: I will divide them in Jacob, and scatter them in Israel."*

Jacob foretold the dishonor and division to the tribe of Levi because of their anger and self-will. The call of God upon Moses would eventually fail because he was not delivered from the family spirit of anger.

Numbers 20:7–12 says, *"And the LORD spoke unto Moses, saying, Take the rod, and gather thou the assembly together, thou, and Aaron thy brother, and speak ye unto the rock before their eyes; and it shall give forth his water, and thou shalt bring forth to them water out of the rock: so thou shalt give the congregation and their beasts drink. And Moses took the rod from before the LORD, as he commanded him. And Moses and Aaron gathered the congregation together before the rock, and he said unto them, Hear now, ye rebels; must we fetch you water out of this rock? And Moses lifted up his hand, and with his rod he smote the rock twice: and the water came out abundantly, and the congregation drank, and their beasts also. And the LORD spoke unto Moses and Aaron, Because ye believed me not, to sanctify me in the eyes of the children of Israel, therefore ye shall not bring this congregation into the land which I have given them."*

God gave Moses specific instructions on how to get water, but because of anger and self-will, Moses spoke angrily to the people and failed to follow what the Lord had commanded him. He struck the rock instead of speaking to it. As a result, the Lord was angry and did not allow him to enter the Promised Land.

King Saul was a man of God born in the clan of Benjamin. The spirit of greed was given access in this tribe, and it destroyed destinies of many. Genesis 49:1 and 27 says, *"And Jacob called unto his sons, and said, Gather yourselves together, that I may tell you that which shall befall you in the last days. Benjamin shall ravin as a wolf: in the morning he shall devour the prey, and at night he shall divide the spoil."*

Jacob foretold the disdain of the tribe of Benjamin, that they shall seek day and night for gain with no satisfaction. Saul had accumulated enough wealth, but the spirit of greed impelled him to get more. He was not delivered from the family spirit of greed.

1 Samuel 9:9,13,18,19, and 26 says, *"But Saul and the people spared Agag, and the best of the sheep, and of the oxen, and of the fatlings, and the lambs, and all that was good, and would not utterly destroy them: but everything that was vile and refuse, that they destroyed utterly. And Samuel came to Saul: and Saul said unto him, Blessed be thou of the LORD: I have performed the commandment of the LORD. And the LORD sent thee on a journey, and said, Go and utterly destroy the sinners the Amalekites, and fight against them*

until they be consumed. Wherefore then didst thou not obey the voice of the LORD, but didst fly upon the spoil, and didst evil in the sight of the LORD? And Samuel said unto Saul, I will not return with thee: for thou hast rejected the word of the LORD, and the LORD hath rejected thee from being king over Israel." The spirit of greed caused Saul's disobedience and failure to obey God's instructions. He failed as king of Israel and also failed his entire generation.

Family spirits are deceptive; manipulating the minds of their victims to think that they are doing the will and commandment of God. Saul could not perceive his lie to Samuel when he told him that he had followed the Lord's commandment. As I struggled with homosexuality and seemed not to get over it, I began considering it as the will of God for my life, which was a deception when we consider God's mind in the holy scriptures.

God was very specific when sending his son Jesus Christ, to earth because he has full knowledge of the effects of family spirits. God chose his son to be born in a family line with no historical family bondage so that he would be able to provide deliverance to those in bondage. Jesus was born to the clan and tribe of Judah.

Genesis 49:8–10 says, *"Judah, thou art he whom thy brethren shall praise: thy hand shall be in the neck of thine enemies; thy father's children shall bow down before thee. Judah is a lion's whelp: from the prey, my son, thou art gone up: he stooped down, he couched as a lion, and as an old lion; who shall rouse him up? The scepter shall not depart from Judah, nor a lawgiver from between his feet, until Shiloh come; and unto him shall the gathering of the people be."*

Jacob spoke triumph to the tribe of Judah: that they will be praised, be overcomers, victorious, rulers, bold, and they will have the laws of God and many positive attributes. All these things happened to Jesus Christ as a member of this tribe.

Coming out of "your father's house" means letting go of family observances and rituals in your father's house that are contrary to the word and principles of God. Some practices are kept secret such that you need to ask God to reveal them to you and also give you an understanding of what is going on in the lives of your relatives. Failure to come out of your father's house will deny you true deliverance.

My father was involved with four women. The first one had no issues according to God's principles, but the second and third were blood sisters while the fourth was from his own clan or bloodline. One of my brothers was a gay porn star; one of my sisters was a street prostitute while my first male lover was from my clan/bloodline. All of these were evidences that the spirit of sexual perversion was active in our lineage.

Ever since the beginning, Satan, through family spirits, has created a system by which he could control families in the entire world, and yet God also wanted Abraham's blessing to start within his family to the families of the world.

Being aware of how family spirits operate is essential to anyone who desires freedom from bondage. They operate intensely in various ways to fulfil their destructive goals, these ways include:

1. Curses: Family spirits cause perversion within a family, and this attracts curses from the Lord. Proverbs 3:33 says, *"The curse of the LORD is in the house of the wicked: but he blesses the habitation of the just."* Different curses, however, affect different areas. For example, a family could be financially blessed yet struggle with the curse of sexual perversion.

Perversions that bring curses in families include:

>   a. Family perversion – polygamous practices, woman being the head of the man, children not submitting to parents, man dishonoring his wife, and others.

>   b. Religious perversion – worshiping anything else rather than the God of heaven through Jesus Christ.

>   c. Sexual perversion – pornography, masturbation, incest, rape, oral sex, drunken sex, anal sex,

bestiality, pedophilia, coprophilia, voyeurism, fornication, adultery, lesbianism, sodomy, lust, phone sex.

d. Financial perversion – financially supporting anything which is against godliness. This also includes stealing; embezzling government funds, cheating on taxes; corruption; giving or taking bribes; selling items that affect people's spiritual, emotional, and physical health (e.g. cigarettes, drugs, pornography, misguided literature or ideologies, dangerous medications, paid sex, dildos, sex machines, sex dolls, etc.)

e. Verbal perversion – speaking anything that is not wholesome, for example: cursing, lies, slander, quarrels, false accusations, flattery, false witnessing, and blasphemy.

f. Behavioral perversion – bad/evil actions which are against God's principles or against others. We need to repent from all perversions in our families and ask God to remove with the blood of Jesus the curses that came along. The Holy Spirit will always guide us on how to break such curses. The Lord wants His children free from these curses. Galatians 3:13 says, *"Christ hath redeemed us from the curse of the law, being made a curse for us: for it is written, Cursed is every one that hangs on a tree."*

2. Purpose: Family spirits have ordained a purpose for each individual in the family to fulfil. It may be to manifest great sexual perversions, great poverty and failure, incurable diseases, mysterious deaths, satanic service, invent wicked social lifestyles, and many other wicked things.

You need to pray and cancel the purpose of these spirits in your life with the blood of Jesus and ask God to bestow his purpose unto your life. 1 John 3:8 says, *"He that commits sin is of the devil; for the devil sins from the beginning. For this purpose the Son of God was manifested, that he might destroy the works of the devil."*

3. Covenant: Family spirits operate legally in one's life through covenants created knowingly or unknowingly. There are eight major satanic covenants in families, and they are: witchcraft covenant, satanic dedication covenant, covenant of attending satanic worship places, sorcery covenant, fornication covenant, satanic financial covenant, covenants with the dead, and satanic verbal covenants.

These covenants must be repented, cancelled through the blood of Jesus, and denounced. Then dedicate yourself or family into the covenant of the blood of Jesus. Cast away every monitoring spirit following such covenants with the blood of Jesus and finally ask God to put his Holy Spirit in you or in your family. Isaiah 28:18 says, *"And your covenant with death shall be disannulled, and your agreement with hell shall not stand."*

Sometimes there are specific rituals and traditions deployed by family spirits to strengthen their covenants within families. Most family members participate in these traditions either knowingly or unknowingly.

This may include eating or avoiding certain foods, wearing particular objects that have been dedicated to these spirits, traditional gatherings to pay tribute to these spirits (dead family members), fornication, abortions, last funeral rites, tattoo wearing, rituals on specific dates or seasons, mandatory circumcisions, newborn baby rituals, ritual sex practices before marriage, dead body rituals, and many others.

4. Laws: Family spirits have rules and regulations that every family member must adhere to. Disobedience usually results in punishment through catastrophes preset by the spirits. Such laws may include restrictions in what you can eat, where you can go, who to marry, what you can possess, and what kind of work you can do.

You need to ask God to break these rules from your life and nail them to his cross. Colossians 2:14 says, *"Blotting out the handwriting of ordinances that was against us, which was contrary to us, and took it out of the way, nailing it to his cross."*

After that, you need to ask God to replace those laws with his law in your life. Psalm 19:7 says, *"The law of the LORD is perfect, converting the soul: the testimony of the LORD is sure, making wise the simple."* Having God's law/principles in your heart is the only thing that can cause conversion of your soul and give you understanding of what is acceptable before God."

Everything God gives to us is preceded by laws or principles if it is to be upheld. These laws could be from scripture or from revelations as the Lord commands us individually with the intention to preserve and prosper us. 1 John 3:22 says, *"And whatsoever we ask, we receive of him, because we keep his commandments, and do those things that are pleasing in his sight."*

5. Secrets: There are hidden secrets in some families for generations, which give family spirits power to control the family. These secrets are protected by the rules given to some specific individuals in the family. Some secrets are hidden in given names while others are hidden in sacred objects that are given to keep or carry on members of the family wherever they go. Such items include sacred water or oil, religious pictures and symbols, pictures or statue of the Virgin Mary or the pope, celebrity pictures, sacred animals or cloths, satanic cultural objects, and many others.

You need to pray about all these things because family spirits may dwell in them and will torment your life if you get rid of them before denouncing their covenants. You need to ask God to reveal these secrets to you so that you know what you are dealing with. Luke 8:17

says, *"For nothing is secret, that shall not be made manifest; neither anything hid, that shall not be known and come abroad."*

6. Gifts: Family spirits can also give gifts or talents to individuals to fulfil Satan's purposes. Isaiah had a gift of cursing tongue, also called false prophecy, and he spoke to fulfill the purposes of these spirits. But one day, Isaiah was delivered from his cursing tongue and received the gift of God. Isaiah 6:5–7 says, *"Then said I, Woe is me! For I am undone; because I am a man of unclean lips, and I dwell in the midst of a people of unclean lips: for mine eyes have seen the King, the LORD of hosts. Then flew one of the seraphim unto me, having a live coal in his hand, which he had taken with the tongs from off the altar: And he laid it upon my mouth, and said, Lo, this hath touched your lips; and your iniquity is taken away, and thy sin purged."*

Gifts from family spirits include; false prophecy, a cursing tongue, lust, romantic eyes, sexy talk and walk, demonic dreams, ability to lure people into sexual perversion, forming perverted music or videos, and many others. Such gifts usually manifest especially after dreaming when we are having a sexual affair with a deceased family member, dreaming when you are at the place you grew up from, dreaming of a dead relative in any context, or a celebrity known for ungodly practices. Such dreams are channels through which family spirits pass on evil mantles from dead relatives or celebrity figures so that we may manifest their demonic lifestyles. The effects of such evil mantles can cause you to fall under the same misfortunes that befell them. Through such dreams, these spirits can also destroy godly mantles in our lives and clothe us with the evil ones. Psalm 143:3 says, *"For the enemy hath persecuted my soul; he hath smitten my life down to the ground; he hath made me to dwell in darkness, as those that have been long dead."*

Immediately after having such a dream, cancel covenants enacted in the dream and dedicate yourself to the covenant of the blood of Jesus. Ask God to tear these evil gifts and evil mantles from you through the blood of Jesus and ask him to replace them with the gifts and mantles of the Holy Spirit to enable you fulfill the purpose of God in your life. Psalm 30:11 says, *"Thou hast turned for me my mourning into dancing: thou hast put off my sackcloth, and girded me with gladness."*

Ephesians 4:8 says, *"Wherefore he says, When he ascended up on high, he led captivity captive, and gave gifts unto men."*

7. Agents: Family spirits have agents who facilitate the fulfillment of the purposes of their gifts and mantles. These agents are people who are usually close to us, like our friends, spouses, counselors, instructors, mentors, idols, trainers, doctors, leaders, etc. And most times, neither the agents nor any of us are aware of the intentions of these spirits.

King Uzziah was used as an agent facilitating Satan's gift within Isaiah to blossom because Uzziah encouraged and believed in Isaiah's deceptive tongue. It was until Uzziah, who is believed to have been Isaiah's cousin, died that Isaiah saw the Lord and acknowledged his deceptive ways. Isaiah 6:1 says, *"In the year that king Uzziah died I saw also the Lord sitting upon a throne, high and lifted up, and his train filled the temple."* Jonadab is another example of an agent used by family spirits when he offered false council to Amnon regarding the lust he had for his sister. The family spirits realized their goal for Amnon, King David's son. Amnon ultimately raped his sister (2 Sam. 13:3–5, 10–14).

Peter the apostle was also used by these spirits to lead his fellow disciples back to the old lifestyle, which Jesus had delivered them from. John 21:2–3 says, *"There were together Simon Peter, and Thomas called Didymus, and Nathanael of Cana in Galilee, and the sons of Zebedee, and two other of his disciples. Simon Peter saith unto them, I go a fishing. They say unto him, We also go with thee. They went forth, and entered into a ship immediately; and that night they caught nothing."*

We should ask God to reveal to us such agents because, most of the time, these people also don't know that they are facilitating the works of evil in other people's lives. Furthermore it's important to ask God to separate them from our lives and frustrate the missions of the family spirits. God can do it in any way he chooses; He can either take them away or guide us out of their circles. Isaiah 44:24–25 says, *"Thus says the LORD, thy redeemer, and he that formed thee from the womb, I am the LORD that makes all things; that stretches forth the heavens alone; that spreads abroad the earth by myself; That frustrates the tokens of the liars, and makes diviners mad; that turns wise men backward, and makes their knowledge foolish."*

Likewise, we should entreat God to bring people who will help us fulfill God's purpose for our lives. Exodus 4:13–15 says, *"And Moses said, O my Lord, send, I pray thee, by the hand of him whom thou wilt send. And the anger of the LORD was kindled against Moses, and he said, Is not Aaron the Levite thy brother? I know that he can speak well. And also, behold, he cometh forth to meet thee: and when he sees you, he will be glad in his heart. And you shall speak unto him, and put words in his mouth: and I will be with thy mouth, and with his mouth, and will teach you what ye shall do."* The Lord sent Aaron to help Moses with the work he had been called for.

8. Networks: Family spirits have a network through which they cause things to occur in people's lives under their control. They are organized in such a way to make people think that the things happening are coincidental, yet they are preplanned.

My first sexual partner lived near my house, yet we met in a place far from my home. In addition, the people I lived with were not at home that particular night when he first came to visit me. The conditions were conducive for action, and this was no coincidence but a preplanned event by the enemy.

Family spirits can create circumstances to get you into trouble and cause one of their agents to show up as a helper, but in the end, it would be a strengthening of their covenant to take you back to their control.

Mark 14:38 says, *"Watch you and pray, lest ye enter into temptation. The spirit truly is ready, but the flesh is weak."* Scripture warns us to pray so that our spiritual eyes may be open to see the networks of the enemy. These should be destroyed daily by your prayers and by the blood of Jesus. You can as well pray that the Lord will show you these networks in dreams and visions to protect you from their traps. Psalm 141:9–10 says, *"Keep me from the snares which they have laid for me, and the gins of the workers of iniquity. Let the wicked fall into their own nets, whilst that I withal escape."*

9. Territories: Family spirits have perimeter walls, uniforms (seals), and guards in the spiritual realm, which keep family members from escaping. Affected family members are usually marked by particular uniformity or a seal of identification. Their walls are invisible yet so real, and their purpose is to keep family members in bondage.

In the physical realm, these walls are represented by things which seem impossible and unattainable unless you obey the rules enforced by the family spirits. The uniformity represents the things or characters common to all affected family members. But because our God is stronger than these spirits, He is able to break down these walls, remove the uniformity, and redeem anyone who agrees to keep his statutes and covenant wholly. Psalm 18:29–30 says, *"For by thee I have run through a troop; and by my God have I leaped over a wall. As for God, his way is perfect: the word of the LORD is tried: he is a bucker to all those that trust in him."* David testifies that God gave him ability to run through the troop [family spirits] and jumped over their wall.

Zechariah 9:11 says, *"As for thee also, by the blood of thy covenant I have sent forth thy prisoners out of the pit wherein is no water."* We should ask the Lord to tear the spiritual uniformity, break the seal, and clothe us in his garment—that is, the fruit of the Holy Spirit—so that we are unrecognizable by these spirits. We also need to ask God to take us out of these territories and destroy their troops so that they cannot take us back into bondage. God can also break the walls as he did with the walls of Jericho. Isaiah 54:3 says, *"For thou shall break forth on the right hand and on the left; and thy seed shall inherit the Gentiles, and make the desolate cities to be inhabited."*

10. Altars: A family usually builds an altar where sacrifices are made to empower family spirits to enforce their purpose in the lives of the family. However, demons and satanic powers are also sent from such altars to attack other family members.

There are people (satanic priests) who consistently attend to these altars and occasionally, every family member is required to take part and serve at the altar or send financial contribution. Sometimes, the priests will call for a family gathering to pray for the spirits of the dead. At such functions, they will prepare certain foods or perform rituals intended to rededicate all family members to these spirits.

During such seasons, we need to pray intensively to destroy these altars with the blood of Jesus, cancel the sacrifices offered, destroy the soul ties (points of contact) used to represent you at the altar, cancel vows made on your behalf, and cut off those powers with the blood of Jesus. Then ask the Holy Spirit to remove your spirit from those altars with the power in the blood of Jesus and take it to the heavenly altar where Jesus is seated.

Judges 6:25–26 says, *"And it came to pass the same night, that the LORD said unto him, Take thy father's young bullock, even the second bullock of seven years old, and throw down the altar of Baal that thy father hath, and cut down the grove that is by it: And build an altar unto the LORD thy God upon the top of this rock, in the ordered place, and take the second bullock, and offer a burnt sacrifice with the wood of the grove which thou shall cut down."*

God instructed Gideon to perform specific tasks to deal with the family spirits in his father's house before serving him. God knew that these spirits are empowered by the satanic altar and can hinder the purposes of God in Gideon's life. God also commanded Gideon to offer a counter sacrifice on God's altar for his entire family's deliverance from bondage.

During those days, they used to offer livestock as sacrifices, but today, God requires only three kinds of sacrifices:

a. **Sacrifice of righteousness**: cleansing your heart of all evil thoughts that are contrary to the fruit of the Holy Spirit. James 3:14–16 says, *"But if ye have bitter envying and strife in your hearts, glory not, and lie not against the truth. This wisdom descends not from above but is earthly, sensual, and devilish."* For where envying and strife is, there is confusion and every evil work. Evil thoughts can be sensual, which means they could have been deposited in our senses by family spirits. Isaiah 55:7 says, *"Let the wicked forsake his way, and the unrighteous man his thoughts: and let him return unto the LORD, and he will have mercy upon him; and to our God, for he will abundantly pardon."* The good thoughts are forgiveness, meekness, love, and many more.

b. **Sacrifice of possessions**: giving some of our possessions to God, to a ministry, or to an individual as led by the spirit of God. Such possessions can be in the form of money, material things, time in praise and worship, holiness (good actions toward people, including your enemies), interceding for others, time to acquire the knowledge of God, raising up hands in prayer, and winning souls as he may ask or reveal to us. Acts 10:1–2 says, *"There was a certain man in Caesarea called Cornelius, a centurion of the band called the Italian band, a devout man and one that feared God with his entire house, which gave much alms to the people, and prayed to God always."* Cornelius's sacrifice was acceptable and God delivered his entire family.

    c. Sacrifice of fasting: denying your flesh the nourishment (food and drink) it needs so that your spirit may be strengthened by the power of God to overcome barriers (forces of darkness) that hinder the will of God in your life, your family, and your community.

Matthew 17:20–21 says, *"And Jesus said unto them, Because of your unbelief: for verily I say unto you, If ye have faith as a grain of mustard seed, ye shall say unto this mountain, Remove hence to yonder place; and it shall remove; and nothing shall be impossible unto you. Howbeit this kind goes not out but by prayer and fasting."* Jesus assured his disciples the necessity of faith to overcome tough situations in life. In addition, Jesus also accentuated the importance of both prayer and fasting to overcome tougher situations.

All these three kinds of sacrifices are made effective through the sacrifice of the blood of Jesus, which we apply to cancel all the sacrifices of the wicked. Proverbs 15:8 says, *"The sacrifice of the wicked is an abomination to the Lord: but the prayer of the upright is his delight."* The blood of Jesus is the platform on which we stand to be accepted before God.

Prayer

Father, in the name of Jesus Christ, I repent all sexual perversions I have introduced into my family line. I repent and cancel with the blood of Jesus all satanic covenants that I and my ancestors entered into. Lord, I repent all things that I have done against you, thinking it was your will.

Lord, forgive me for every evil thought in my heart and wash them away with the blood of Jesus. Give me a new heart to walk with you.

Lord, I dedicate my names in the blood of Jesus, and I denounce all satanic covenants attached to my names. I cut off every evil spirit, evil prophecy, and evil character that have been following me to fulfill their desired destiny because of my names. Let my names be cleansed with the blood of Jesus and be blessed to represent your purposes in my life.

Lord, in the name of Jesus, I repent all perversions that have caused curses upon us on behalf of my family. Lord, remove these curses from our family with the blood of your son, Jesus Christ, and let the blessing of Abraham come upon us in Jesus's name.

Lord, I cancel every purpose my family spirits have in my life with the blood of Jesus, and I ask you, Lord, to bestow your purpose unto me.

Lord, I repent all satanic covenants operating within my family. I cancel and denounce all forms of covenants on witchcraft, covenants dedicated to demons, covenants for attending satanic worship places, covenants on sorcery, covenants for fornication, covenants on satanic finances, covenants on satanic utterances, covenants with the dead by the blood of Jesus Christ.

Lord, I dedicate my life and family on the covenant with the blood of Jesus and ask you to deliver us through this covenant out of all satanic pits in Jesus's mighty name.

Lord, I cast out all family spirits by the blood of Jesus and let your Holy Spirit fill their place in our family. In Jesus's name.

Lord, I ask you to break all family spirits rules within my family; put them out of our way by nailing them to your cross. Put your laws, oh Lord, into our hearts so that we may be converted in Jesus's name.

Lord, I ask you to reveal the secrets of the family spirits in our family; open my understanding to see the objects I have been keeping and through which these spirits have been connecting with me.

Lord, I cancel all covenants I enacted in dreams with the dead people, with celebrities, and of sexual encounters. I ask you to remove their mantles and gifts from my spirit with the blood of Jesus. I dedicate my life to the covenant with the blood of Jesus, and I ask you to replace all satanic mantles and gifts with the mantle of the Holy Spirit in Jesus's name.

Lord, I ask you to reveal family spirit agents in my life, separate them from me with the heaven's chariots of fire, make them mad, and frustrate all their tokens and missions through the blood of Jesus. Turn them backward and make their knowledge into foolishness in Jesus's mighty name.

Lord, I ask you to open my spiritual eyes to see the networking of the family spirits in my life, I destroy all their networks with the blood of Jesus, bring their counsel to nothing, and deactivate their plans for my life. Keep me from their snares and temptations; let only your counsel stand in my life in Jesus's name.

Lord, in Jesus's name, I ask you to tear the uniformity and seals of family spirits from my life with the blood of Jesus; replace them with the garment and seal of the Holy Spirit. Discomfit all their troops and break their spiritual demarcations with the blood of Jesus so that I may escape into your mighty hand in Jesus's name.

Lord, in the name of Jesus, I cancel with the blood of Jesus all kinds of sacrifices, which have been offered to the family spirits on my behalf. I offer the blood of Jesus as my counter sacrifice at God's altar in heaven, whose blood speaks of better things than the blood they offered on the behalf of my family. I destroy all points of contact that have been representing me on those altars with the fire of God. I throw down those altars and denounce all vows made on my behalf. I destroy all powers attacking me from those altars with the blood of Jesus Christ. Lord, deliver my spirit, soul, and body from the hands of family spirits with your stretched-out arm and bring me to your heavenly altar forever. Lord, restore whatever family spirits had taken or denied us sevenfold in Jesus's mighty name. Amen.

7

Does My Geographical Location Matter?

The spirit of sexual perversion can choose to take control over an extensive area and manifest in the residents' lifestyles in that area. Such areas may vary from a unit household to an entire continent. The main avenues of influence of this spirit of lust in the lives of residents may include their cultures, the way they dress, their language, and their systems of governance. My initial signs of sexual perversion manifested when I was attending an all-boys high school, which had an atmosphere conducive for its proliferation.

When the spirit selects an area, it will manifest in people's lives without discriminating against age, gender, race, income level, educational level, or faith or religion. This happened to the people who lived in Sodom and its neighboring cities, including those who had recently relocated to this city. The new dwellers' lifestyle were influenced either by means of seduction or forced sex— if it wasn't already in their bloodline.

Genesis 19:4–5 says, *"But before they lay down, the men of the city, even the men of Sodom, compassed the house round, both old and young, all the people from every quarter. And they called unto Lot, and said unto him, where are the men which came in to thee this night? Bring them out unto us, that we may have sexual relations with them."*

It was not by coincidence that the young and old in the city were well aware of the men who had just come into the city. This is indicative of the spirit of sexual perversion traversing the whole city to make sure that everyone is marked and is under its control.

The people of Gibeah were also under control of the same spirit. They were accustomed to God's laws concerning homosexuality but did not have the ability to change their ways because of the spiritual enforcement of this spirit.

Judges 19:15–16, 21–22 says, *"And they turned aside thither, to go in and to lodge in Gibeah: and when he went in, he sat him down in a street of the city: for there was no man that took them into his house to lodging. And, behold, there came an old man from his work out of the field at even, which was also of mount Ephraim; and he sojourned in Gibeah: but the men of the place were Benjamites. So he brought him into his house, and gave provender unto the asses: and they washed their feet, and did eat and drink. Now as they were making their hearts merry, behold, the men of the city, certain sons of Belial, beset the house round about, and beat at the door, and spoke to the master of the house, the old man, saying, Bring forth the man that came into your house, that we may know (have sexual relations with) him."*

We should realize that evil spirits can subdue the children of God and cause them to lead corrupt lifestyles. God warns us to be aware of such influence caused by the wicked spirit in our places of abode. Psalm 125:3 says, *"For the rod [control] of the wicked [spirit] shall not rest upon the lot [geographical location] of the righteous; lest the righteous put forth their hands unto iniquity."*

God gives clear instructions to all his people on what to do in every new location they move to. The scripture in Jeremiah 29:7 says, *"And seek the peace of the city whither I have caused you to be carried away captives, and pray unto the LORD for it: for in the peace thereof shall ye have peace."*

The Lord reminds us to pray to Him specifically regarding our new locations to avoid the control of the spiritual forces in these places. When we pray to God about our countries or neighborhoods, he will take control and we shall live in peace. Isaiah 25:7–8 says, *"And he will destroy in this mountain the face of the covering cast over all people, and the veil that is spread over all nations. He will swallow up death in victory; and the Lord God will wipe away tears from off all faces; and the rebuke of His people shall he take away from off all the earth: for the LORD hath spoken it."*

Territorial spirits create an obscure covering over God's people in their demarcated locations, inflicting pain in the lives of the people. This also brings a reproach on them, but God promises to destroy such spiritual coverings when his people pray against them. Psalm 101:8 says, *"I will early destroy all the wicked (controlling spirits) of the land; that I may cut off all wicked doers from the city of the Lord."* After praying, we need to declare the word of God upon our locations. Psalm 24:1 declares, *"The earth is the Lord's, and the fullness thereof; the world, and they that dwell therein."*

The beach used to be my favorite location for a date with a guy. The environment suited my lifestyle, and there was a lot of homosexual activities. Today, we have cities, towns, recreational parks, streets, organizations, schools, hotels, campuses, churches, apartments, and beaches that are under the control of this spirit of sexual perversion and its very active in the lives of its residents.

Jeremiah 11:13 says, *"For according to the number of thy cities were thy gods [controlling spirits], O Judah; and according to the number of the streets of Jerusalem have you set up altars [perverted lifestyle locations] to that shameful thing, even altars to burn incense [to practice wicked lifestyles] unto Baal."* God is talking about cities, streets, and altars erected to worship Baal. Their worship included the sacrifice of unborn babies (abortion), indulging in heterosexual and homosexual immorality among the worshippers, and giving special reverence to nature. This spirit of sexual perversion demands the same activities from all those that are under its control.

There are also people in these demarcated locations who work as priests or mediums who promote or sponsor the works of the controlling spirits. Such people are usually influential in politics, business, music arts, sports, spirituality and many more. These people must be dealt with in prayer to cut off their influence. Ezekiel 11:1–2, 4, 13 says, *"Moreover, the spirit lifted me up, and brought me unto the east gate of the Lord's house, which looks eastward: and behold at the door of the gate twenty five men; among whom I saw Jaazaniah the son of Azur, and Pelatiah the son of Benaiah, princes of the people. Then said he unto me, Son of man, these are the men that devise mischief, and give wicked counsel in this city: Therefore prophesy against them, prophesy, O son of man. And it came to pass, when I prophesied, that Pelatiah the son of Benaiah died. Then fell I down upon my face, and cried with a loud voice, and said, Ah Lord God! wilt thou make a full end of the remnant of Israel?"*

We don't kill people using prayer, but we kill their influence spiritually if it propagates perversion in our areas.

Prayer

Father, in the name of Jesus, I dedicate my city and residents to the blood of Jesus. We repent of all sin and all perversions caused by the spiritual covering over us.

Forgive us and cleanse us of sexual perversions with the blood of Jesus. Lord, destroy that spiritual covering with the blood of Jesus along with all it's effects in this city. Let the kingdom of God come and take control, and let it be over us. Let it break the kingdom of darkness and sexual perversion into pieces.

Lord, come and break the scepter of the wicked over this place so that the righteous will flourish In the name of Jesus.

Father, this city, its residents, and everything in it belong to you. Therefore, we spiritually cut off all the wicked on the land and cast them out of this city along with their influence. We destroy all altars that propagate perversion with the blood of Jesus and ask you to set up the kingdom of God in this location to rule over the people by wiping away their tears and removing the reproach of sexual perversion from them in Jesus's mighty name.

We declare that this city belongs to God Almighty, and his reign shall be forever through Jesus Christ, our Lord. Amen.

8

Who Bewitched You?

In my search for deliverance from homosexuality, I asked God to reveal to me exactly what my problem was. The Lord showed me that I had unknowingly visited a false prophet's church that put a spell of sorcery upon me, and this caused part of my bondage. At this point, its when I realized that it is possible for one to be bewitched into homosexuality and other forms of sexual perversion. Christians can be bewitched when God's covenant is weakened in their lives through ignorance, spiritual weakness, pride, fear, unforgiveness, sin (evil thoughts, evil utterances, and evil deeds). Numbers 23:19–21 says, *"God is not a man, that He should lie; neither the son of man, that He should repent: hath He said, and shall he not do it? or hath He spoken, and shall he not make it good? Behold, I have received commandment to bless: and He hath blessed; and I cannot reverse it. He hath not beheld iniquity in Jacob, neither hath He seen perverseness in Israel: the LORD his God is with him, and the shout of a king is among them."*

The only reason why Israel could not be bewitched was because God neither saw iniquity nor perverseness in them unlike in many Christians today. Numbers 23:23 says, *"Surely there is no enchantment against Jacob, neither is there any divination against Israel: according to this time it shall be said of Jacob and of Israel, What hath God wrought!"*

It is very hard to understand the root of the bizarre feelings of attraction you get toward those of the same gender when you are bewitched into sexual perversion. This kind of witchcraft can be used by people who want to lure you into their businesses, like prostitution, strip clubs, false churches, and various forms of adult entertainment. Such spells of witchcraft will cause the victim to do whatever the director demands without fear or shame and disregarding their own reputation, families, and friends. Victims can also go nude and do abominable acts in public places or on camera, on televised commercials, at beaches, at schools, places of worship, at bachelor and bachelorette parties, and many more.

Another sign of witchcraft can be a sudden change in behavior or beliefs, departing from the moral truth and toward deception. In most cases, you will find that such victims will support things they used to detest when they were still in their normal senses. I remember one time when I pondered on the thought of how outrageous it was for a guy to want to sleep with a fellow guy. However, when I fell under the spell of witchcraft, it felt attractive, and I was proud of my homosexual relationships.

In scripture, we see a certain man who used witchcraft on the entire city, and the residents believed him to be a man of God. Acts 8:9–11 says, *"But there was a certain man, called Simon, which beforetime in the same city used sorcery, and bewitched the people of Samaria, giving out that himself was some great one: To whom they all gave heed, from the least to the greatest, saying, This man is the great power of God. And to him they had regard, because that of long time he had bewitched them with sorceries."*

Simon's sorcery caused those he bewitched to take heed and to regard and respect him as someone blessed by God with a supernatural ability or talent, exactly as we see porn stars today.

This kind of attitude is very similar to how I regarded porn stars. I saw them as great people and respected them for their bodies, talent, and supernatural presentation. I did not realize that I was under the influence of the witchcraft spells they use on their clients and audiences.

Such spells can be transferred using a point of contact which may include a piece of clothing: your name; a photo; a video; and personal items like under garments, bedsheets, menstrual pads, hair, fingernails, jewelry, sexual objects (dildos, rubber, vibrators, sensual oils and creams), etc. These items represent you at the altar of the spirits of sexual perversion from where they send spells to influence your lifestyle.

On the contrary, you can also be bewitched by receiving or purchasing items, including gifts, food, and drinks, which have spells on them. Some of these can be very attractive and expensive such that you feel privileged to receive them, yet the outcome would be displeasing. Furthermore, body piercings and tattoos can carry on them demonic spells. Leviticus 19:28 says, *"You shall not make any cuttings in your flesh for the dead, nor print any marks upon you: I am the Lord."*

In a religious setting, one can be bewitched; by the laying of hands, by so-called sacred items with sorcery spells on them or by being anointed with oil from the person who is bewitching you. Sexual perversion through witchcraft causes you to often dream of the person who did it to you.

We overcome such sorceries by first inviting Jesus Christ into our lives because He alone has the power over witchcraft. Acts 8:12–13 says, *"But when they believed Philip preaching the things concerning the kingdom of God, and the name of Jesus Christ, they were baptized, both men and women. Then Simon himself believed also: and when he was baptized, he continued with Philip, and wondered, beholding the miracles and signs which were done."*

Simon (the sorcerer) gave his life to Jesus Christ and continued in fellowship with Philip. This is the call to everyone who is, or has been, a victim of sorcery. Next, we have to repent opening our lives to sorcery through ignorance, spiritual weakness, sin (bad thoughts, bad words and deeds), pride, fear, and unforgiveness. Forgive the person who bewitched you by asking God to give you his spirit of forgiveness to enable you to totally forgive. Do not curse or seek revenge with hatred, envy, and anger.

Pray for the person by repenting on their behalf for all they have done to you. Dedicate them to the blood of Jesus and cancel the covenants of sorcery they had dedicated you to. Ask the Lord Jesus to have legal rights over them through his blood and declare the spirit of conviction and truth into their lives so as to change them. Dedicate yourself also to the blood of Jesus and cancel any other satanic covenants that may be operating in your life. Put on the blood of Jesus, the power and authority of God. Then cast out the spirit that has been causing sexual perversion with the blood of Jesus and the word of God because that spirit cannot operate within the spheres of the blood of Jesus. Deuteronomy 23:17 says, *"There shall be no whore of the daughters of Israel, nor a sodomite of the sons of Israel."* After expelling it out of your heart, mind, and body, invite the Holy Spirit to take its place and, lastly, declare victory against it. Job 22:27–29 says, *"Thou shall make thy prayer unto him, and he shall hear thee, and thou shall pay thy vows. Thou shall also decree a thing, and it shall be established unto thee: and the light shall shine upon thy ways."*

The Lord will hear our prayers, and we will keep our vows by walking in his ways.

Finally, you need to declare what you want to happen in your life, and it shall be established. This is when you declare, "I am no longer sexually perverse in Jesus's mighty name," and it will be so.

Prayer

Father, in the name of Jesus Christ, I repent all evil thoughts, words, and deeds that I have done and those done on my behalf. Lord, forgive me and wash me in the blood of Jesus; erase my name from the book of the dead and write it in the lamb's book of life. Fill me with your Holy Spirit to guide me all the days of my life in Jesus's mighty name. Amen.

Father, I repent opening my life to sorcery through my ignorance, spiritual weakness, sin, pride, fear, and unforgiveness. Cleanse me from all these with the blood of Jesus.

Lord, I forgive every person who bewitched me, and I ask you to give me your spirit so that I may have the ability to forgive genuinely. On behalf of that person, we repent for practicing sorcery under the influence of evil spirits and deception. Lord, I dedicate everyone who has bewitched me to the blood covenant of Jesus Christ that you may have legal authority over them. Bless them and open their understanding to the conviction of the Holy Spirit against deception. Remove the spirit of deception and clothe them with your spirit of truth to guide them toward repentance.

Lord, I repent and cancel all covenants of sorcery in which I was dedicated with the blood of Jesus. I dedicate my life to the blood covenant of Jesus Christ and cancel all other satanic covenants, of witchcraft, of dedication, and of fornication that have been operating in my life with the blood of Jesus.

Right now, I cover myself, my loved ones, and all my stuff in the blood of Jesus. I put on the power of God and the authority of his word. I drag all spirits of sorceries and sexual perversions into the blood of Jesus, and I expel them out of my life, my heart, my mind, and my body, never to come back in Jesus's name. It is written there shall be no sorceries against me because I am now a child of God. Holy Spirit, come into my life and replace all sorceries with your presence in Jesus's name. I declare I am no longer a homosexual in Jesus's name. Amen.

9

The Eye Connection

The eyes are one of the gateways to the soul and, therefore the easiest point of entry for the spirit of sexual perversion into your soul. This spirit will cause you to desire looking at something seductive to arouse your senses whenever it wants to take control of your mind.

In time, you lose control of yourself when you focus on the stimulant, and that is when this spirit takes charge. Stimulants may include pornography, music videos, and audio recordings, which cause your mind to create corresponding images to what you see and hear.

Someone partially dressed in, like sagging pants, tight pants, transparent clothing, clothes with holes, or garments that give an indication that one does not have any undergarments on act as stimulants. Some sports gear is so seductive and a great trap, which this spirit uses to get into your senses, if your mind thinks through what you are looking at. For this reason you need to control what you watch.

The spirit of sexual perversion makes pleasant what your eyes see and intensifies the desire to see more. It does not take long for one to be possessed and acquire the passion to do things that were previously undesirable. This was the same trick Satan used to influence Adam and Eve's lives. Genesis 3:6–7 says, *"And when the woman saw that the tree was good for food, and that it was pleasant to the eyes, and a tree to be desired to make one wise, she took of the fruit thereof, and did eat, and gave also unto her husband with her; and he did eat. And the eyes of them both were opened, and they knew that they were naked; and they sewed fig leaves together, and made themselves aprons."*

Satan's main mission in your life is to open your eyes to see what he sees so that you become one with him. This allows him access to your entire body (feelings and senses). Jesus in Luke 11:34 says, *"The light of the body is the eye: therefore when your eye is single, thy whole body also is full of light; but when your eye is evil, thy body also is full of darkness."* This implies that when your eye watches and brings in evil (sexual perverseness), it will circulate the entire body and subdue it.

Becoming one with the devil means that you acquire the same desires of the spirit of sexual perversion. Your feelings and senses are totally defiled and the things that were previously unacceptable start feeling good and desirable.

This is similar to what happened to my life. I took interest in what my first partner was watching. I liked what I saw; it felt pleasant to my eyes. Just like Eve, I took and ate because it looked good.

Satan did not hesitate to tempt Jesus. Luke 4:3 says, *"And when the tempter came to him, he said, if thou be the Son of God, command that these stones be made bread."* Satan wanted Jesus to look at those stones as bread. But thank God that Jesus was very aware of Satan and his operations in people's lives. Jesus did not accept seeing the way Satan sees.

The truth was that these were stones, but Satan wanted Jesus to see them as bread, but because he knew the Word, he therefore quoted the scriptures. God never considered stones as bread, and he did not have to consult with anyone about this. Had Jesus agreed to see the stones as bread, it would have been so for the rest of his life.

From the time I looked at pornographic materials, I began seeing guys as potential sexual partners. I had pornographic pictures and videos on my cellphone because this kind of material had become pleasant to my eyes and desirable sexual food. That is why Jesus asks us to pay attention to what we watch. Matthew 5:28 says, *"But I say unto you, that whosoever looks on a woman [creation] to lust after her has committed adultery [sexual perversion] with her already in his heart."* We have seen the eye opening up the body, and now it also opens up the heart to receive what it brings in.

The heart processes what the eyes lust after, and the body will follow with a response action. Lamentations 3:51 says, *"Mine eye affects mine heart because of all the daughters of my city."* The writer acknowledges the effect the lust of his eyes has on his heart whenever he looks at the girls in the city; his heart is defiled.

Job made a pact with his eyes never to look lustfully at a woman. Job 31:1 says, *"I made a covenant with mine eyes; why then should I think upon a maid?"* King David also made a decision not to look at any pornographic productions and expressed disdain for those who dealt crookedly with it, and he wanted nothing to do with them. Psalm 101:3 says, *"I will set no wicked thing before mine eyes: I hate the work [perverted sexual productions] of them that turn aside; it shall not cleave to me."*

Paul tells us that the spirit of lust will blind your spiritual eyes and we will not be able to see God's will for our lives. Before my deliverance, I used to get dreams where my eyes were partially blind. Dreams are a reflection of what we really are in God's sight. We need to ask God for spiritual eyes to see as he sees us. Jesus opened so many physically blind eyes in his ministry to show us that he will open so many of us who are spiritually blind in this generation.

2 Corinthians 4:3–4 says, *"But if our gospel be hid, it is hid to them that are lost: in whom the god of this world hath blinded the minds of them which believe not, lest the light of the glorious gospel of Christ, who is the image of God, should shine unto them."*

You may be having a good life as seen by physical eyes yet wretched spiritually. Revelation 3:17–18 says, *"Because thou sayest, I am rich, and increased with goods, and have need of nothing; and knowest not that thou art wretched, and miserable, and poor, and blind, and naked. I counsel thee to buy of me gold tried in the fire, that thou mayest be rich; and white raiment, that thou mayest be clothed, and that the shame of thy nakedness do not appear; and anoint thine eyes with eye salve, that thou mayest see."*

In addition, you may be going through hard times as showed through the physical eyes, yet you are victorious spiritually. Revelation 2:9 says, *"I know thy works, and tribulation, and poverty, [but thou art rich] and I know the blasphemy of them which say they are Jews, and are not, but are the synagogue of Satan."*

I wrestled with scripture after my heart, feelings, and senses were defiled by sexual perversion. I could not find a preacher who agreed with my corrupted nature nor the scripture translations to give me some form of comfort in my defilement. I started doubting whether scripture was inspired by God, yet 2 Timothy 3:16–17 says, *"All scripture is given by inspiration of God, and is profitable for doctrine, for reproof, for correction, for instruction in righteousness: That the man of God may be perfect, thoroughly furnished unto all good works."*

My mind eventually became permeated with pornographic images, which constantly played in my mind whenever I closed my eyes in prayer. This made me feel so filthy to pray. I started hating prayers and attending church. I imagine the psalmist could have been in a similar situation when he prayed in Psalm 119:37, saying, *"Turn away mine eyes from beholding vanity; and quicken thou me in thy way."* I urgently needed revival to avoid the grave.

Lot and his family received clear instructions from the angels not to look back when they delivered them from the destruction in Sodom to avoid being consumed. The angels knew that looking back would impede their great deliverance. Unfortunately, Lot's wife disobeyed and looked back; she became a pillar of salt.

Genesis 19:17 and 26 says, *"And it came to pass, when they had brought them forth abroad, that he said, escape for thy life; look not behind thee, neither stay thou in all the plain; escape to the mountain, lest thou be consumed." But his wife looked back from behind her, and she became a pillar of salt.*

This is happening often among the many who God has delivered. They watch and think about things that remind them of previous perverted lifestyles, which resurrect the cycle of spiritual blindness and breed sexual perversion again.

Prayer

Father, in the name of Jesus, I repent all doors I have opened for the spirit of sexual perversion to my eyes. Forgive me and wash my spiritual and physical eyes with the blood of Jesus so that I may be delivered from the bondage of sexual perversion.

Lord, I repent and cancel all covenants with the spirit of sexual perversion in my eyes with the blood of Jesus. I dedicate my eyes to the covenant of your blood and cast out every spirit that entered my heart and body through them. Lord, touch my eyes. Revive me that I may see as you see. Holy Spirit, come and sit on my eyes and turn them away from beholding vanity in Jesus's mighty name. Amen.

10

I Cannot Bear It Any Longer

A time came in my life when I really became tired of the homosexual lifestyle. I felt insulted and had no privacy due to the multiple sexual partners. I was overwhelmed by my brother's agony as HIV/AIDS devoured his body. The money he earned as a gay porn star could not help him at all. I had to endure the shame that I bore in the Christian community after my ex-wife left due to my gay lifestyle. In addition, I was faced with the uncertainty of not knowing what was going to happen to my three-year-old son. My burden was heavy.

I was so hard-pressed that I came to a point of harboring suicidal thoughts, yet the sense of where I would spend eternity if I did what I thought was quite scary. I wanted to get out of this pain but did not know how to change it from temporary relief to an eternal one.

Jude 1:7 says, *"Even as Sodom and Gomorrah, and the cities about them in like manner, giving themselves over to fornication, and going after strange flesh, are set forth for an example, suffering the vengeance of eternal fire."* If the pain I had was terrible for a few months, how much more would it be to have it eternally?

The only option I was left with was to cry out to God for help. The Lord answered my desperation in a dream of the night when someone told me about a deliverance minister who could help me out of my perversion. I have come to understand that God will help anyone who gets tired of carrying their burdens and reaches out to him for help.

Matthew 11:28 says, *"Come unto me, all you that labor and are heavy laden, and I will give you rest."* It is only through our actions of faith where we express disdain for our evil ways that the Lord will intervene.

The Lord promised His friend, Abraham, that his seed will be delivered after four hundred years of slavery. But after four hundred years, the Hebrews did not do anything about their bondage to express their pain. It was after another thirty years that they groaned and cried out to God. Then God remembered that his friend Abraham had paid for them through his obedience and sent them a deliverer.

Exodus 2:23–24 says, *"And it came to pass in process of time that the king of Egypt died: and the children of Israel sighed by reason of the bondage, and they cried, and their cry came up unto God by reason of the bondage. And God heard their groaning, and God remembered his covenant with Abraham, with Isaac, and with Jacob."*

The same also applies to us today. In obedience to His father, Jesus died on the cross to pay the price on our behalf for us to receive God's blessings. However, we can only access these blessings through our obedience to the instructions of the covenant, which include crying out for help when we are heavily laden. The whole world receives God's blessings because of Jesus's obedience to his Father.

Hebrews 10:36 says, *"For you have need of patience, that, after you have done the will of God, you might receive the promise."*

In His earthly ministry, Jesus had compassion for the people who were burdened and came to Him for solutions. He saw their determination from what they had to loose to get to him and by the instructions of the covenant which they were able to obey.

Luke 17:11–14 says, *"And it came to pass, as he went to Jerusalem that he passed through the midst of Samaria and Galilee. And as he entered into a certain village, there met him ten men that were lepers, which stood afar off: And they lifted up their voices, and said, Jesus,*

Master, have mercy on us. And when he saw them, he said unto them, Go show yourselves unto the priests. And it came to pass, that, as they went, they were cleansed."

A person tired of their circumstances or bondage is usually willing to follow instructions by their redeemer. Likewise, the Lord knows a person who is weary and heavy-laden by their willingness to carry Jesus's burden of instructions. It is through obedience that we get rest because the Lord's burden is lighter than the devil's.

Matthew 11:29–30 says, *"Take my yoke upon you, and learn of me; for I am meek and lowly in heart: and you shall find rest unto your souls. For my yoke is easy, and my burden is light."*

When the Lord told me about the minister he had anointed for my deliverance, I obeyed and went to his church. When I reached there, I received another instruction to tell him exactly what was going on in my perverted lifestyle, and when I did, I was cleansed and became whole again. The Lord sent angels to deliver Lot from the perversion in Sodom with specific instructions which he had to follow to acquire his deliverance.

Genesis 19:17 and 22 says, *"And it came to pass, when they had brought them forth abroad, that he said, Escape for thy life; look not behind thee, neither stay thou in all the plain; escape to the mountain, lest thou be consumed. Haste you, escape from here; for I cannot do anything till you be come there. Therefore the name of the city was called Zoar."*

There are three categories of people in Lot's family. First is Lot and his virgin daughters who obeyed all instructions and received total deliverance. Secondly is Lot's wife who partially obeyed and was overthrown on her way to total deliverance.

Genesis 19:26 says, *"But his wife looked back from behind him, and she became a pillar of salt."* This is when we look back to the temporal benefits we enjoyed in sexual perversion and we covet them hence turning back. Thirdly, Lot's sons-in-law who saw the instructions as a mockery and disobeyed all of them and were destroyed in the city.

Genesis 19:14 says, *"And Lot went out, and spoke unto his sons in law, which married his daughters, and said, up, get you out of this place; for the LORD will destroy this city. But he seemed as one that mocked unto his sons in law."*

We each belong to one of the three categories above, and that's what we portray to the world. The purpose of this book is to present the instructions of our covenant with the God of Abraham toward receiving total deliverance from perverted sexual lifestyles.

Prayer

Father, in the name of Jesus Christ, I ask you to give me the burden of getting tired of the sexual perversion in my life.

Give me the opportunity to understand your instructions for my deliverance so that I may follow all of them till I am totally delivered.

Lord, don't allow the enemy to deceive me into thinking that even if I don't follow the instructions, I would get better by mockery.

Please give me the power of your Holy Spirit to follow you to total deliverance. In Jesus's mighty name. Amen.

11

Swiftness

After acquiring the necessary knowledge to confront the spirit of sexual perversion, you must desire for a complete change in your life. Procrastination is a tool commonly presented by this spirit to destroy its victims. You need to understand that this same spirit is aware of your newly acquired knowledge, and it will create circumstances and use anybody to delay or make sure that you do not achieve your freedom from bondage.

When Israel was battling this spirit of sexual perversion among the children of Benjamin, it was made known to the Benjamites what Israel had planned and so it is today. Judges 20:3 says, *"[Now the children of Benjamin heard that the children of Israel were gone up to Mizpeh.] Then said the children of Israel, Tell us, how was this wickedness?"*

If you are planning to repent your sexual perversion to receive your freedom, then you need to do it now wherever you are. Many have lost their lives because of procrastination, uncertain of when they really want to repent.

I recall the day I had plans to attend a deliverance service on a Tuesday night with my friend Chris (the guy God used for my deliverance). We had agreed that I would give him a call and meet up downtown to go to the service since I didn't know the address of the church.

I got to downtown through public means, and when I reached for my phone in my pocket, I realized that it was missing and, therefore, could not call him. Fortunately, there was a pay phone close, but I did not have Chris's number in my memory. However, I recalled a cell number of one of his friends whom I asked to contact Chris on my behalf. A few minutes later, I called him back to confirm whether he had spoken to Chris, but to add to my distress, he told me that his phone froze and suddenly deleted all his contacts! I felt like I was battling something within my spirit, so real but yet invisible. Though I did not understand what was going on, I was determined to get to church against all odds. This is the kind of zeal that God wants everyone who is determined to repent to have.

Isaiah 37:32 says, *"For out of Jerusalem shall go forth a remnant, and they that escape out of mount Zion: the zeal of the Lord of hosts shall do this."*

We thank God that he always makes a way of escape whenever we pursue righteousness. He did it for the children of Israel as they fled from Egypt. He did it throughout scripture and is still doing it today.

I then decided to go to the taxi hub because I was determined not to be hindered by any disappointments. To my great surprise, within earshot, I heard taxi operators calling out on the top of their voices, "Mutundwe Christian Fellowship, Pastor Tom." And at that point, I remembered that my friend Chris had mentioned that name. I hurriedly boarded one of the taxis that was going to Pastor Tom's church, and that's where my entire life took a complete turn never to be the same.

The spirit of sexual perversion gives great zeal to its victims in doing unimaginable actions without shame or fear even in public. Christians need to perform God's work with greater zeal from the Lord.

When the angels came to Sodom to deliver Lot and his family from the judgment that was due, Lot was overcome by procrastination. Genesis 19:15–16 says, *"And when the morning arose, then the angels hastened Lot, saying, Arise, take thy wife, and thy two daughters, which are here; lest thou be consumed in the iniquity of the city. And while he lingered, the men laid hold upon his hand and upon the hand of his wife, and upon the hand of his two daughters; the LORD being merciful unto him: and they brought him forth, and set him without the city."*

Apostle Paul had a great door opened before him for effective ministry, but the enemy put up many challenges against him. The enemy will always create resistance for anyone who pursues godliness. 1 Corinthians 16:9 says, *"For a great door and effectual is opened unto me, and there are many adversaries."* Circumstances, including urgent appointments, job offers, uninvited guests, accidents, sickness, or even a flat tire, may happen to hinder your deliverance; therefore, you should be aware. When such things happen, many people will think it's God behind them when the reality is that the enemy is fighting spiritual freedom.

1 Thessalonians 2:18 says, *"Wherefore we would have come unto you, even I Paul, once and again; but Satan hindered us."*

Many would be free from sexual perversion today, but this spirit has hindered them in various ways, including false reports about God's ministers who would have otherwise helped them or the body of Christ as a whole.

When King David realized the enemy in his own house, he advised everyone around him to leave the city immediately lest they perish. I also advise anyone battling the spirit of sexual perversion to expeditiously cancel any plans and events that promote this spirit if you are to save your life.

2 Samuel 15:14 says, *"And David said unto all his servants that were with him at Jerusalem, Arise, and let us flee; for we shall not else escape from Absalom: make speed to depart, lest he overtake us suddenly, and bring evil upon us, and smite the city with the edge of the sword."*

We saw earlier that this spirit will do anything to hinder your freedom, but your determination will move God to send you help from above. This is evident in scripture when Jesus was heading to the other side of the sea to free a man who was controlled by a group of evil spirits.

These spirits created a storm on the sea to hinder or destroy Jesus before he could reach the man at the other side. But thank God that Jesus was familiar with the spirits' tactics and prevailed against them.

Mark 4:37–39 says, *"And there arose a great storm of wind, and the waves beat into the ship, so that it was now full. And he was in the hinder part of the ship, asleep on a pillow: and they awake him, and say unto him, Master, cares thou not that we perish? And he arose, and rebuked the wind, and said unto the sea, Peace, be still. And the wind ceased, and there was a great calm."*

Mark 5:1–3 says, *"And they came over unto the other side of the sea, into the country of the Gadarenes. And when he was come out of the ship, immediately there met him out of the tombs a man with an unclean spirit, Who had his dwelling among the tombs; and no man could bind him, no, not with chains."*

The disciples woke Jesus from his sleep, and he rebuked the storm (the hindrance), and they were able to get to the man who needed deliverance. When you realize that your deliverance is being hindered, then you need to ask the Lord for help. I pray that Jesus rebukes every hindrance to your deliverance and use you also to remove hindrances in other people's lives, those who need deliverance in Jesus's name.

Prayer

Father, in the name of Jesus, I pray that you forgive me for procrastination when it comes to the things of God yet so quick in things related to sexual perversion.

Lord, cleanse me from all spirits of deception that hinder my deliverance through the blood of Jesus.

Lord, give me the zeal of God in my spirit so that I may perform God's will with boldness and without delay.

Lord, open my eyes to see all disguises of the spirit of sexual perversion in people and in circumstances.

Lord, send me help from above to remove every hindrance out of my way so that I can realize my deliverance. In Jesus's mighty name. Amen.

12

My Blood Was Shed in Vain

A true story is told of a certain man who had the opportunity to visit heaven in a vision. He saw the Lord Jesus crying because the church was losing the battle on earth against evil spirits, yet it had the greatest weapon, His blood. In anguish, Jesus said these words, "My blood was shed in vain if the church does not understand it or know how to use it."

Secrets of the Blood of Jesus

There are only two people who have lived on earth who had the origin of their blood direct from God without any impurity (sin). Adam and Jesus's blood were not from any male, and therefore, it was pure. Adam's blood became defiled when he was tempted to sin while Jesus's blood remained pure because he did not succumb to temptation. This qualified Jesus's blood to save the human race and atone for it's sin.

People offer blood sacrifices to evil spirits to atone for their lives' bad circumstances, hoping for a better life. The size of the sacrifice determines the strength of the blood. However, in the spiritual world, it is the strength of the blood offered that determines the victor.

2 Kings 3:26–27 says, *"And when the king of Moab saw that the battle was too sore for him, he took with him seven hundred men that*

drew swords, to break through even unto the king of Edom: but they could not. Then he took his eldest son that should have reigned in his stead, and offered him for a burnt offering upon the wall. And there was great indignation against Israel: and they departed from him, and returned to their own land."

In this contest, Israel, who are a people of God, lost the battle to a heathen king because he offered a bigger sacrifice than them. Various blood sacrifices include; blood of birds, blood of animals, blood of human beings usually the firstborn male children or princes. In addition, living sacrifices can be made where people are subjected to pain until death.

God knows the secret of sacrifice, and He designed the ultimate sacrifice for His church. God's ultimate sacrifice is three-fold in one. Jesus, the firstborn of God and heavenly prince, was offered as a living sacrifice on the cross. The purity of Jesus's blood qualifies it to be the strongest sacrifice ever. Understanding the power of sacrifice will give you a victorious life as a Christian.

I used to plead for the blood of Jesus for myself and my partner before and after each sexual affair. Based on false teachings previously received, I thought that the blood of Jesus would cover us so that God will see us through Jesus's blood and not acknowledge our sin. It was after I was delivered that I came to understand that the blood of Jesus is a covenant blood that only works when you are in covenant with God.

Luke 22:20–22 says, *"Likewise also the cup after supper, saying, this cup is the New Testament in my blood, which is shed for you. But, behold, the hand of him that betrays me is with me on the table. And truly the Son of man goes, as it was determined: but woe unto that man by whom he is betrayed."*

Jesus introduced the blood to his disciples and besought them to stay in covenant with Him. Jesus continued to tell them that someone was going to betray him and will receive the wages of his actions if he doesn't change his mind (repent).

I was exactly like Judas Iscariot. I knew what I was planning to do with my sexual partners. If the blood I pleaded could not change my mind and turn me away from my plans, that was proof that I had broken my covenant with the Lord of the blood.

The presence of the blood didn't hinder Jesus from seeing the sin in Judas. Neither did it stop the wages of his actions. The blood of Jesus is effective when one truly repents and enters into a covenant with the God of the blood. We seek true repentance and ask for forgiveness for our sins through the blood of Jesus. Colossians 1:14 says, *"In whom we have redemption through his blood, even the forgiveness of sins."* The blood does not cover the sin but washes it away so that the person will not sin again.

Hebrews 9:14 says, *"How much more shall the blood of Christ, who through the eternal Spirit offered himself without spot to God, purge your conscience from dead works to serve the living God?"*

Purging prepares you for service to the living God. My previous lifestyle, preaching and singing in the choir, was a disservice to God. I asked the Lord to wash away homosexual feelings from my heart and purchase me from the hand of the spirit of sexual perversion in my prayer for deliverance.

The Benefits of the Blood of Jesus to the Believer

A. Purchases: The blood of Jesus purchases you from the hand of the evil one as it did for the children of Israel from the hand of the pharaoh in Egypt.

Acts 20:28 says, *"Take heed therefore unto yourselves, and to all the flock, over the which the Holy Ghost hath made you overseers, to feed the church of God, which he has purchased with his own blood."*

Washing with blood takes place after you have been purchased, because you cannot wash something that does not belong to you. God purchased the children of Israel with the blood of the lamb and then later washed them in the Red Sea. The Red Sea represents the blood of Jesus, which also destroyed the Egyptians that followed after them to bring them back to bondage (old lifestyles).

1 Peter 1:18–19 says, *"Forasmuch as you know that you were not redeemed with corruptible things, as silver and gold, from your vain conversation received by tradition from your fathers; But with the precious blood of Christ, as of a lamb without blemish and without spot."*

B. Washes: The blood of Jesus washes our spiritual garments clean of every stain and makes them white. Every good or bad activity in our lives appears as a garment in the spiritual realm; therefore, it is very important to often wash our garments with the blood of Jesus. Our garments can be stained by the sin we commit or by spells (curse words) spoken by evil people at us.

In my prayer for deliverance, I confessed that "I wash sexual perversion out of my garments by the blood of Jesus Christ."

Revelation 7:14 says, *"And I said unto him, Sir, thou knowest. And he said to me, These are they which came out of great tribulation, and have washed their robes, and made them white in the blood of the Lamb."*

The saints who are going to appear before the Lord are those who have gone through this filthy world and washed the filthiness of this world from their garments with the blood of Jesus.

C. Cancels Covenants: The blood of Jesus cancels all demonic covenants that brought us into bondage. Sex is a covenant between you, your sexual partner, and their gods. Exodus 23:32–33 says, *"Thou shalt make no covenant with them [perverted sexual partners], nor with their gods [spirits of sexual perversion]. They shall not dwell in thy land [spirit, soul and body], lest they make thee sin against me: for if thou serve their gods, it will surely be a snare [prison] unto thee."*

God cannot operate in your life unless He has a covenant with you, and so does Satan. We need to repent our covenants with Satan, which brought us into bondage, and cancel them with the blood of Jesus and then enter into a covenant with God to receive our deliverance. After this, we can ask the Lord to deliver us from the prison of sexual perversion.

Zechariah 9:11 says, *"As for thee also, by the blood of thy covenant I have sent forth thy prisoners out of the pit wherein is no water."*

D. Detoxicate: The spirits of sexual perversion will still pursue you after your deliverance with the intention of bringing you back into bondage. You need to continue sprinkling the blood of Jesus to destroy them from your mind and feelings.

Revelation 12:11 says, *"And they overcame him by the blood of the Lamb, and by the word of their testimony; and they loved not their lives unto the death."*

We overcome the spirit of sexual perversion with the blood of Jesus and our own confession with the word of God against it. We also apply the blood to destroy it's affection in our heart.

The Lord Jesus is able, through his blood, to make you hate the evil you adored, and the devil is able, through his spirits, to force you do something you detest. I have met many people who previously hated homosexuality yet they enjoy it today, and many who previously enjoyed homosexuality yet hate it today. All this is a result of whichever spirit is controlling your life, either the Holy Spirit or the spirit of sexual perversion.

Philippians 3:7–8 says, *"But what things were gain to me, those I counted loss for Christ. Yea doubtless, and I count all things but loss for the Excellency of the knowledge of Christ Jesus my Lord: for whom I have suffered the loss of all things, and do count them but dung, that I may win Christ."* After accepting Jesus and getting deliverance, Apostle Paul considered his former lifestyle as dung (poo-poo) compared to what he gained by knowing Jesus as his Lord.

E. Atone: The blood of Jesus atones for our souls in the process of deliverance. When we ask for the atonement through the blood of Jesus, we are asking that the blood of Jesus will replace our souls at the dock of captivity. This works as a bail bond given in court to release the defendant.

Leviticus 17:11 says, *"For the life of the flesh is in the blood: and I have given it to you upon the altar to make an atonement for your souls: for it is the blood that makes an atonement for the soul."*

Souls held captive at the spiritual altars of the spirit of sexual perversion can only be bailed with the blood of Jesus. It is very important that you ask the Lord to atone for your soul with the blood of Jesus.

F. Advocate: The blood of Jesus is an advocate that speaks of better things on our behalf in the process of deliverance. There are verbal covenants we have made or were made (by our ancestors) on our behalf without our knowledge through the words uttered to the spirit of sexual perversion which have to be cancelled.

The words we usually speak in intimate moments are vows we make to the spirit of sexual perversion that resides in your sexual partner. Expressions, such as, "I will love you forever"; "I am your boy"; "We will stay together for life"; "Nothing will ever separate us"; "you are the best thing in my life"; "If you ever leave me, I will die"; "Without you I am lifeless"; "I am at your service"; "You own my soul"; and so many others will pursue you for fulfilment. The spirit of sexual perversion will hold you to your words and keep you in bondage. Proverbs 6:2 says, *"Thou art snared with the words of thy mouth, thou art taken with the words of thy mouth."*

Galatians 3:15 says, *"Brethren, I speak after the manner of men; Though it be but a man's covenant, yet if it be confirmed, no man disannuls, or adds thereto."*

You can only nullify your words (vows) after such covenants with the blood of Jesus that has the power to set you free. Hebrews 12:24 says, *"And you have come to Jesus the mediator of the new covenant, and to the blood of sprinkling, that speaks better things than that of Abel."*

Blood that is shed during sexual affairs is a sacrificial offering for that covenant, and it is that blood that speaks about perversion in our lives constantly. It is therefore important to ask the Lord for his blood to speak of better things (like deliverance, restoration, cleansing, and blessing) on your behalf.

G. Draw us: The blood of Jesus brings us near to God and causes us to enjoy His true presence again. Our spirits come from God's presence into the womb of our mothers. But because we sinned, the presence of God was cut off from us so that we no longer share his presence and character. We took on the presence of evil spirits and also share their character. Romans 3:23 says, *"For all have sinned, and come short of the glory of God."*

Ephesians 2:13 says, *"But now in Christ Jesus ye who sometimes were far off are made nigh by the blood of Christ."* Hebrews 10:19–20 says, *"Having therefore, brethren, boldness to enter into the holiest by the blood of Jesus, By a new and living way, which he hath consecrated for us, through the veil, that is to say, his flesh."*

H. Purge: The blood of Jesus purges us of dead works or weaknesses so that we may serve the living God. Serving God while having evil lifestyles rescinds (disqualifies) our service. Therefore, it is important for us to ask the Lord to purge our hearts, minds, and bodies with his blood of all works that are contrary to our true service to Him.

Hebrews 9:14 says, *"How much more shall the blood of Christ, who through the eternal Spirit offered himself without spot to God, purge your conscience from dead works to serve the living God?"*

I.   Unify: The blood of Jesus unites us with the Lord such that he enters and abides in us the same way the spirit of sexual perversion has been abiding in us. The blood will fight for God's place in our lives by casting out every intruder who desires to dwell in us. God is holy; He cannot dwell with anything unholy in our heart, mind, and body.

John 6:56 says, *"He that eats my flesh, and drinks my blood, dwells in me, and I in him."* It is important to confess that "I drink the blood of Jesus to remove the spirit of sexual perversion from me so that the spirit of Jesus will enter and abide in me."

J.   Protect: The blood of Jesus is a shield of protection for us and our substances against the attacks of evil spirits. Whenever we cast out the evil spirits from our lives, they will try to harm our lives, offspring, finances, marriages, ministries, properties, loved ones, or anything important to us. But we should always cover our everything with the blood of Jesus. The spirit of sexual perversion has tried and still tries to harm me and my substances even after my deliverance. I always cover myself (whether awake or sleeping), my family, my transportation (vehicle or flight), my meals (food or drinks), my clothing, my wife (from any affair), and substances in the blood of Jesus against such attacks. The blood of Jesus can protect you from sexually transmitted infections if your spouse hasn't been faithful and contracted one.

Exodus 12:13 says, *"And the blood shall be to you for a token upon the houses where ye are: and when I see the blood, I will pass over you, and the plague shall not be upon you to destroy you, when I smite the land of Egypt."*

Prayer

Father, in the name of Jesus, I repent all sexual perversions that have happened in my spirit, soul, and body. Let the blood of your son, Jesus Christ, bring forgiveness into my life.

Lord, I invite the blood of Jesus into my life to purchase me from the custody of the spirit of sexual perversion and bring me back to you, Lord Jesus Christ.

Lord, I soak my garments in the blood of Jesus and let it wash away all spots and spells of perversion from my garments and make them white.

Lord, I repent and cancel all evil covenants with the spirits of perversion with the blood of Jesus. I dedicate my life to the blood of your covenant, and I ask you to take me from every prison where I am bound in Jesus's name.

Lord, I drink the blood of Jesus so that it detoxicates me and causes me to hate sexual perversion.

Lord, I ask you to atone for my soul with the blood of Jesus and remove it from the sexual perversion altar where it has been held captive.

Lord, I repent all the words and vows I have made with the spirit of sexual perversion and its agents. I cancel all of them with the blood of Jesus. Let this blood speak of deliverance in my life in Jesus's name.

Lord, let the blood of Jesus bring me back into the presence of God and purge my conscience of all dead works so that I may serve the living God.

Lord, let the blood of Jesus unite me with you so that I live in you and you in me and so that whoever fights me will be fighting you.

Lord, I cover my life, my loved ones, and everything that belongs to me in the blood of Jesus for our protection and permanent deliverance. In Jesus's mighty name. Amen.

13

True Repentance

I knew that my life as a homosexual was not pleasing in God's sight. My consciousness was a witness to that at the beginning until the false teachings I took in suppressed my guilt, and I became comfortable with zero conviction.

1 Timothy 4:1 says, *"Now the Spirit speaks expressly, that in the latter times some shall depart from the faith, giving heed to seducing spirits, and doctrines of devils; Speaking lies in hypocrisy; having their conscience seared with a hot iron."*

It was impossible for me to repent after my consciousness being defiled. I had no reason to repent for something I was taught and believed was God-given. It was after I learned the real truth about sexual perversion that my spiritual conviction was restored.

Sin can be categorized as follows:

A. Known sin: This is acknowledged sin yet you don't have the strength to quit. James 4:17 says, *"Therefore to him that knows to do good, and doeth it not, to him it is sin."*

B. Unknown sin: Inadvertent, not being aware that your actions hurt God. God expects us to ask him whether we are doing His will. Satan will always do his best to hide sin in us, but remember, ignorance of the law excuses no one.

Psalm 19:12–13 says, *"Who can understand his errors? cleanse thou me from secret faults. Keep back thy servant also from presumptuous sins; let them not have dominion over me: then shall I be upright, and I shall be innocent from the great transgression."*

   C. Double-minded: A state of mixed feelings, enjoying worldly stuff (secular entertainment, drinking, immorality, smoking) and at the same time enjoying the things of God (church music, charity work, volunteering, partnering with ministries).

Revelation 3:15–16 says, *"I know thy works, that thou art neither cold nor hot: I would thou wert cold or hot. So then because thou art lukewarm, and neither cold nor hot, will I spew thee out of my mouth."*

True repentance begins with acknowledging your sin and its effects on the heart of God. All bondage or evil addictions are a result of sin, which must be uncovered for one to receive total freedom. In many cases, the enemy deceives us by convincing us that "it is too many of us in this practice to all be wrong," and the enemy will also twist the scriptures through misinterpretation to keep us in bondage.

Lamentations 2:14–15 says, *"Thy prophets have seen vain and foolish things for thee: and they have not discovered your iniquity, to turn away thy captivity; but have seen for thee false burdens and causes of banishment. All that pass by clap their hands at thee; they hiss and wag their head at the daughter of Jerusalem, saying, is this the city that men call the perfection of beauty, the joy of the whole earth?"*

Many people are caught up in false teachings, causing them to stay in sexual perversion's captivity, which sometimes is referred to as the joy of the whole earth. Nonetheless, God gives us enough time to regain our consciousness and repent before He reproves us.

Psalm 50:17–18, 21 God says, *"Seeing you hate instruction, and cast my words behind you. When you saw a thief, then you consented with him, and you have been a partaker with adulterers. These things you have done, and I kept silence; you thought that I was altogether such an one as thyself: but I will reprove you, and set them in order before your eyes."*

It is always the deceptive doctrines that cause us to take God for granted, but by His mercy, He will find a way to get the truth to us, and after which, judgment will proceed.

John 15:22 says, *"If I had not come and spoken unto them, they had not had sin: but now they have no excuse for their sin."*

My ministry, marriage, and finances were booming during the fifteen years of sexual perversion, and I had favor with everyone. I traveled extensively for ministry appointments until one day when evil struck. God can use a calamity (a heart break, a great financial need, an incurable disease, loss of job or property, imprisonment, death of loved one) to get your attention.

2 Chronicles 33:10–13 says, *"And the LORD spoke to Manasseh, and to his people: but they would not hearken. Wherefore the LORD brought upon them the captains of the host of the king of Assyria, which took Manasseh among the thorns, and bound him with fetters, and carried him to Babylon. And when he was in affliction, he besought the LORD his God, and humbled himself greatly before the God of his fathers, and prayed unto him: and he was entreated of him, and heard his supplication, and brought him again to Jerusalem into his kingdom. Then Manasseh knew that the LORD he was God."*

Many of us wait for affliction before we seek God for help as King Manasseh did. As for me, it was a misunderstanding between me and my boss, which resulted in losing my job that got my attention back to God. Secondly, I lost my marriage when my ex-wife learned about my unfaithfulness. Thirdly, my ministry partners learned about the cause of my marriage breakdown, and they abandoned me. Finally, I lost my social status when my sexual perversion became public.

I went into depression and became suicidal instead of seeking godly help. I hated God for allowing all this to happen. The enemy's goal was to kill me before I could make it up to my creator, but I thank God for the one true friend (Chris) who stayed with me and showed me the way back to God.

I pray that through this book, I would be a true friend to show you the way back to your creator. You do not need to wait much longer for something catastrophic to happen to you. God has a limited time in which he expects you to turn back to Him.

After the death of King Manasseh, his son took over the kingship and walked into the same sins as his father. He did not turn back to God but sinned more and more until he was murdered in the course of his sin.

2 Chronicles 33:20–24 says, *"So Manasseh slept with his fathers, and they buried him in his own house: and Amon his son reigned in his stead. Amon was two and twenty years old when he began to reign, and reigned two years in Jerusalem. But he did that which was evil in the sight of the LORD, as did Manasseh his father: for Amon sacrificed unto all the carved images which Manasseh his father had made, and served them; And humbled not himself before the LORD, as Manasseh his father had humbled himself; but Amon trespassed more and more. And his servants conspired against him, and slew him in his own house."*

You are subject to eternal rejection when your appointed time to repent lapses. You can be rejected forever and be delivered to one with a mind of a reprobate who will never allow you to repent until death. Romans 1:28 says, *"And even as they did not like to retain God in their knowledge, God gave them over to a reprobate mind, to do those things which are not convenient."*

Hebrews 12:16–17 says, *"Lest there be any fornicator, or profane person, as Esau, who for one morsel of meat sold his birthright. For you know how that afterward, when he would have inherited the blessing, he was rejected: for he found no place of repentance, though he sought it carefully with tears."*

Furthermore, Hebrews 4:7 says, *"Again, he limits a certain day, saying in David, to day, after so long a time; as it is said, today if ye will hear his voice, harden not your hearts."*

Prophet Samuel's prayers could not restore Saul as king of Israel because his time for restoration had elapsed. 1 Samuel 16:1 says, *"And the LORD said unto Samuel, How long will you mourn for Saul, seeing I have rejected him from reigning over Israel? Fill your horn with oil, and go, I will send you to Jesse the Bethlehemite: for I have provided Me a king among his sons."*

True repentance begins with acknowledging that you are walking in sin. The spirit of the Lord will convict you by opening your senses to the truth.

John 16:7–8 says, *"Nevertheless I tell you the truth; It is expedient for you that I go away: for if I go not away, the Comforter will not come unto you; but if I depart, I will send him unto you. And when he is come, he will reprove the world of sin, and of righteousness, and of judgment."*

You need to bear the fruit of repentance after conviction. This means you should feel sorrow and be ashamed of your sin. Most people never feel sorry for their sins but only hide them so that no one is aware of their challenges.

The day I visited the ministry, which the Lord used to deliver me, the preacher read Proverbs 28:13–14, which says, *"He that covers his sins shall not prosper: but whosoever confesses and forsakes them shall have mercy. Happy is the man that fears always: but he that hardens his heart shall fall into mischief."*

When I heard these words, I heard a voice on the inside, saying, "To the extent you've hidden your sexual perversion, the more you have become filthy, but if you confess it today, I am going to deliver you." I was already sorrowful about the actions I had done in the past fifteen years. I felt so bad for the guys I had seduced into homosexuality, using my position as a leader, yet I was supposed to be their protection. I did not feel that I deserved mercy, but it was at my disposal, and I had to do something to receive it. I had to confess and forsake my sin. Matthew 3:5–8 says, *"Then went out to him Jerusalem, and all Judaea, and all the region round about Jordan, And were baptized of him in Jordan, confessing their sins. But when he saw many of the Pharisees and Sadducees come to his baptism, he said unto them, O generation of vipers, who hath warned you to flee from the wrath to come? Bring forth therefore fruits meet for repentance."* The fruit of repentance is the sorrow you get in your heart that causes you to detest your sin and have a complete turn around.

Your sorrow must be birthed with the conviction of you sinning against such a patient God. This kind of sorrow produces true repentance and makes you become very careful not to sin again. It will also lead you to separate yourself from everything or any person who promotes that sin (sexual perversion).

True repentance also continues to bring the fear of God into your heart, knowing that God punishes us for the sin in our lives.

2 Corinthians 7:10–11 says, *"For godly sorrow works repentance to salvation not to be repented of: but the sorrow of the world works death. For behold this selfsame thing, that ye sorrowed after a godly sort, what carefulness it wrought in you, yea, what clearing of yourselves, yea, what indignation, yea, what fear, yea, what vehement desire, yea, what zeal, yea, what revenge! In all things ye have approved yourselves to be clear in this matter."*

Godly sorrow for your sexual perversion will allow you to confess your sins and get yourself salvation. Simple or worldly confession will not result in your forgiveness, neither will it produce transformation.

After confessing your sin before God, you need to ask Jesus to wash and cleanse you with His blood. Psalm 51:7 says, *"Purge me with hyssop, and I shall be clean: wash me, and I shall be whiter than snow."* In the Old Testament, hyssop was used to wash sinners clean, but today we use the blood of Jesus.

Some deeply rooted familial sins (perversions) can be persistent even after repentance. Such sins need to be blotted out through prayer and fasting like tough stains in a garment that can only be removed by very strong chemicals.

Matthew 17:19–21 says, *"Then came the disciples to Jesus apart, and said, Why could not we cast him out? And Jesus said unto them, Because of your unbelief: for verily I say unto you, If ye have faith as a grain of mustard seed, ye shall say unto this mountain, Remove hence to yonder place; and it shall remove; and nothing shall be impossible unto you. Howbeit this kind goes not out but by prayer and fasting."*

As you repent, ask the Lord to remove the defiled heart and the evil spirit, which has been causing that particular sin, and ask him to give you a new, clean heart with the spirit of God to avoid slipping back into sin.

Ezekiel 18:30–31 says, *"Therefore I will judge you, O house of Israel, every one according to his ways, says the Lord God. Repent, and turn yourselves from all your transgressions; so iniquity shall not be your ruin. Cast away from you all your transgressions, whereby you have transgressed; and make you a new heart and a new spirit: for why will you die O house of Israel?"*

God requires us to turn away from our transgressions (sexual perversion) and not allow iniquity (repeated perversions) to continue because it will ruin our lives. The new heart from God will cause you to forsake and hate the sin. Your new heart will also help you stand with others, helping them to get out of perversion.

After getting a new heart, ask the Lord to restore His joy within your heart. You will start feeling free and will surely enjoy your new life with Christ. David asked God for a new heart after repenting his adultery. He also vowed, after receiving a new heart, that he would teach other adulterers the ways of the Lord and lead them to repentance.

Psalm 51:8–13 says, *"Make me to hear joy and gladness; that the bones which thou hast broken may rejoice. Hide thy face from my sins, and blot out all mine iniquities. Create in me a clean heart, O God; and renew a right spirit within me. Cast me not away from thy presence; and take not thy Holy Spirit from me. Restore unto me the joy of thy salvation; and uphold me with thy free spirit. Then will I teach transgressors thy ways; and sinners shall be converted unto thee."*

The story of the prodigal son is a reflection of how God responds to those who truly repent. God is merciful and full of grace, which means that he has pity for the sinner, and his grace restores all that they lost due to sin in their life. True repentance (which happens in the heart) precedes confession(which happens with the mouth), then God restores the sinner.

Luke 15:17–24 says, *"And when he came to himself, he said, How many hired servants of my father's have bread enough and to spare, and I perish with hunger! I will arise and go to my father, and will say unto him, Father; I have sinned against heaven, and before thee, And am no more worthy to be called thy son: make me as one of thy hired servants. And he arose, and came to his father. But when he was yet a great way off, his father saw him, and had compassion, and ran, and fell on his neck, and kissed him. And the son said unto him, Father, I have sinned against heaven, and in thy sight, and am no more worthy to be called thy son. But the father said to his servants, Bring forth the best robe, and put it on him; and put a ring on his hand, and shoes on his feet: And bring hither the fatted calf, and kill it; and let us eat, and be merry: For this my son was dead, and is alive again; he was lost, and is found. And they began to be merry."*

This teaches us that God can see true repentance from afar and will move to embrace anyone determined to confess. The prodigal son started with feeling sorrowful about his sin and reflecting on the pain he had caused in his father's heart. Whenever we confess our sin after repentance in the heart, God restores double for the sins we forsake.

Isaiah 40:1–2 says, *"Comfort you, comfort you my people, says your God. Speak you comfortably to Jerusalem, and cry unto her, that her warfare is accomplished, that her iniquity is pardoned: for she hath received of the LORD'S hand double for all her sins."*

God restores blessings upon a person after their sin is pardoned. However, such blessings and grace (supernatural abilities) upon you can cause others who have not truly repented to become envious and also think that God is not fair.

Luke 15:25–28 says, *"Now his elder son was in the field: and as he came and drew nigh to the house, he heard music and dancing. And he called one of the servants, and asked what these things meant. And he said unto him, Thy brother is come; and thy father hath killed the fatted calf, because he hath received him safe and sound. And he was angry, and would not go in: therefore came his father out, and entreated him."*

After I truly repented, God gave me another ministry, a new marriage, new ministry partners, more true friends, and he is opening greater doors and opportunities, which have made many envious.

Every sin causes a curse upon our lives, and the curse opens a door for demons to operate in our lives. These demons will bring us to satanic covenants, which will give Satan legal ground to do whatever he wills in our lives. We therefore need to repent of any sin (sexual perversion), ask Jesus to redeem us from the curses (curse of sexual perversion), cancel satanic covenants (covenant of fornication), and cast out the evils spirits (Jezebel and her children) that have been operating through the curses.

All these should be replaced with righteousness, which will cause a blessing to come into our lives. The blessing will open up a door for the Holy Spirit to operate within us freely, bringing us into a stronger covenant with Jesus Christ. The godly covenant will give God legal ground to do all his will in our lives.

Prayer

Father, in the name of Jesus, I come before you and ask you to convict me of any sin and perversion that have caused pain in your heart. Give me to sorrow after a godly pattern.

Lord, make my sin known to me so that I may be able to repent truly.

Lord, through the blood of Jesus, I thrust out all false teachings which have suffocated my consciousness that I can no longer feel your convictions.

Lord, I repent for being double-minded, which has caused me to be between two opinions, enjoying both godly and worldly stuff.

Lord, I repent not listening to your warnings I have always received until evil has stricken me. I ask you for the grace to genuinely repent in my heart and to turn away from the evil way.

Lord, I confess my sin and ask you to forgive me for all the sexual perversions I have walked in. Wash away all my sin with the blood of your son, Jesus Christ.

Lord, blot out all engraved family perversions from me and give me the ability to fast because I know that this kind doesn't go except through prayer and fasting.

Lord, give me also the fruit of repentance in my heart so I never turn back to sexual perversion.

Lord, remove from me that defiled heart and give me a new heart with a new spirit in the name of Jesus Christ.

Lord, restore unto me the joy of thy salvation and uphold me with thy free spirit.

Help me, Lord, to teach others your way so that they may be converted to you.

Lord Jesus, I ask you to redeem me from every curse that came as result of sexual perversion.

Lord, I repent and cancel all satanic covenants on fornication with the blood of Jesus and dedicate my life into the blood covenant of the Lord Jesus.

Lord, I ask you to remove that spirit of Jezebel out of my life with the blood of Jesus and fill me with your Holy Spirit.

Lord, restore your blessing in my life that I may glorify your name in Jesus's mighty name. Amen.

14

Seeds Will Grow

After true repentance, you become aware of the initial seeds planted by the enemy that brought forth the plant of sexual perversion. Perversion begins as a seed is planted. It grows roots and later, it brings branches. The process of growth in the ground (heart) is not evident above the ground until the branches (actions) grow, then the plant (sexual perversion) will manifest. This is true with the kingdom of God.

Mark 4:30–32 says, *"And he said, whereunto shall we liken the kingdom of God? or with what comparison shall we compare it? It is like a grain of mustard seed, which, when it is sown in the earth, is less than all the seeds that be in the earth: But when it is sown, it grows up, and becomes greater than all herbs, and shoots out great branches; so that the fowls of the air may lodge under the shadow of it."*

This scripture illustrates the process by which spiritual things manifest in the physical. This cautions us to pay more attention to what is going on in our heart, mind, and body.

When Are Seeds Sown?

Seeds of sexual perversion are sown when we are not aware and, therefore, are not easily detected.

Matthew 13:25 says, *"Another parable put Jesus forth unto them, saying, The kingdom of heaven is likened unto a man which sowed good seed in his field: But while men slept, his enemy came and sowed tares among the wheat, and went his way. But when the blade was sprung up, and brought forth fruit, then appeared the tares also."* So seeds are sown when men are asleep, meaning when the owner of the field least expects it.

My first sexual affair was at age eight when I was molested by our female nanny, and the seed was sown. At that time, I did not understand the extent of what happened, and due to poor communication with my dad and step mum, I did not share it with anyone.

Please understand that the enemy will take advantage of your innocence to sow seeds, and that is why God commands us to sow godly seeds in our children.

Proverbs 22:6 says, *"Train up a child in the way he should go: and when he is old, he will not depart from it."* Training a child is comparable to sowing. Anything good or evil sown in you as a child will eventually grow.

Where are seeds sown?

Seeds of sexual perversion, including other seeds, are primarily sown in the three parts of our being: the spirit (your heart), soul (contains your mind), and body (contains your senses). These seeds will grow and defile different areas of your being accordingly:

I.   Spiritual life – satanic seeds will cause an inability to discern spiritually what is godly.
II. Marriage life – seeds will cause an inability to choose a suitable partner who would enhance the purposes of God in your life.
III. Financial life – seeds will cause you to be unable to establish godly provision for your life and will connect you

to abominable provisions, which will lure you into deeper sexual perversion.

IV. Health – these seeds will cause health problems that cannot be fixed by regular physicians without the Lord's intervention.

V. Ministry – these seeds in a ministry will generate corrupt and perverted ministers and believers.

VI. Offspring – these seeds will defile your offspring so that they cannot attain their God-given destiny.

How Are Seeds Sown?

Seeds of sexual perversion are sown in various ways, including:

1. Lineage – When there was sexual perversion in one or more people in your lineage. Such seeds can only be uprooted by the Lord through his blood as he promised to do so if we come to him whole heartedly.
   Joel 3:21 says, *"For I will cleanse their blood that I have not cleansed: for the LORD dwells in Zion."*

2. Love for money – The enemy can entice you with money or material possessions during your time of financial distress to get you into sexual perversion.
   1 Timothy 6:10 says, *"For the love of money is the root of all evil: which while some coveted after, they have erred from the faith, and pierced themselves through with many sorrows."*

3. Abuse – Seeds of self-rejection can be sown when one is abused for no particular reason. After self-rejection, the enemy will make you feel worthless and entice you into sexual perversion as you seek for acceptance and care.
   Obadiah 1:13–15 says, *"Thou should not have entered into the gate of my people in the day of their calamity; yea, thou should not have looked on their affliction in the day of their calamity, nor have laid hands on their substance in the day of their calamity; neither should thou have stood in the*

crossway, to cut off those of his that did escape; neither should thou have delivered up those of his that did remain in the day of distress. For the day of the LORD is near upon all the heathen: as thou hast done, it shall be done unto thee: thy reward shall return upon your own head." This is God's warning towards everyone who abuses others.

4. Molestation – Seeds can be sown through sexual molestation or by being seduced as a minor. This route is commonly used by the enemy because he knows that the seeds will grow as the person grows. Molestation usually breeds bitterness and unforgiveness in your heart. Ultimately, these will also cause you to desire revenge on anyone who may be vulnerable. Hebrews 12:15–16 says, *"Looking diligently lest any man fail of the grace of God; lest any root of bitterness springing up trouble you, and thereby many be defiled. Lest there be any fornicator or profane person as Esau, who, for one morsel of meat, sold his birthright."*

5. Name – Seeds of sexual perversion can also be sown in one's life through their given name or nickname. A name derived from another person who struggled with sexual perversion is an identity and carries the desired character(s) of that person. In addition, the intention of your name could be for you to become the meaning of the name.

   What you call yourself or what others call you is very important. This may be due to your behavior, body build, how you dress, the tone of voice, and others. However, if you have a name that connects you to sexual perversion in any way, you need to change it or sanctify it with the blood of Jesus to receive total freedom.

   Genesis 27:36 says, *"And he said, Is not he rightly named Jacob? for he hath supplanted me these two times: he took away my birthright; and, behold, now he hath taken away my blessing. And he said, Hast thou not reserved a blessing for me?"* All my given names were derived from a chief who had various sexual perversions, and these names got me in so much trouble until I dropped them.

1 Samuel 25:25 says, *"Let not my lord, I pray thee, regard this man of Belial, even Nabal: for as his name is, so is he; Nabal is his name, and folly is with him."*

6. Religion and traditional beliefs – Seeds of sexual perversions sown through what you have been raised to believe in or your religion will make you walk in sin with zeal, thinking that you are doing your creator a service.

   Galatians 1:13–14 says, *"For ye have heard of my conversation in time past in the Jews' religion, how that beyond measure I persecuted the church of God, and wasted it: And profited in the Jews' religion above many my equals in mine own nation, being more exceedingly zealous of the traditions of my fathers."*

   Apostle Paul did many evil things because he believed he was fulfilling the requirements of his religion and his father's traditions.

7. Dreams – Seeds of sexual perversions can also be sown by the enemy through sexual dreams whereby demons of perversion teach you what they want you to do. I constantly had dreams while I was sleeping with men and saw their private parts. By the time I woke up, I would be so lustful, feeling the push to go and practice what I saw in the dream. Most people think these are mere dreams, but they are actual seeds being sown within our spirit by the enemy. Dreams are a means of communication with the spiritual realm, and they will indicate bondage or freedom.

   Deuteronomy 23:10 says, *"If there be among you any man, that is not clean by reason of uncleanness that happens to him by night[in a dream], then shall he go abroad out of the camp, he shall not come within the camp."*

8. Pornographic materials – Seeds of sexual perversion are largely sown by pornographic movies, pictures, music videos, video games, kids' movies, and reading materials. All these

will play scenes in your mind, causing demonic spirits of perversion to enter through your eyes as we saw earlier in one of the chapters. I was a victim of this route, and I know great multitudes have also been captivated. You will realize today that most secular videos and movies have a sexual scene with the intention of sowing seeds.

Psalm 101:3 says, *"I will set no wicked thing before mine eyes: I hate the work of them that turn aside; it shall not cleave to me."*

9. Music – Music is one of the greatest channels through which seeds of sexual perversions are sown. This music carries an impartation of sexual perversion from the person singing to the people listening to their music.

    2 Kings 3:15 says, *"But now bring me a minstrel [music minister]. And it came to pass, when the minstrel played, that the hand of the LORD came upon him."*

10. Laying of hands – a sexually perverse person can sow seeds of sexual perversion into your life when they lay their hands on you in prayer. Likewise, a spiritually clean person sows godly seeds into your life when they lay hands on you in prayer.

    2 Timothy 1:6 says, *"Wherefore I put thee in remembrance that thou stir up the gift of God, which is in thee by the putting on of my hands."* At the laying on of hands people receive gifts either from God or from Satan.

11. Conversations – Seeds of sexual perversion can be sown when we engage in immoral conversations that arouse sexual feelings. Seeds of sexual perversion were also sown in my life during the conversation I had with a friend about homosexuality at the café. It was then that I began to develop feelings for him.

    2 Peter 2:6–8 says, *"And turning the cities of Sodom and Gomorrah into ashes condemned them with an overthrow, making them an ensample unto those that after should live ungodly; And delivered just Lot, vexed with the filthy*

conversation of the wicked: [For that righteous man dwelling among them, in seeing and hearing, vexed his righteous soul from day to day with their unlawful deeds.]"

12. Food – Seeds of sexual perversion can also be sown through what we feed our bodies. Drinks, food, medications, body fluids like blood, and body organs where spells of sexual perversion have been cast on are supposed to be sanctified through prayer and the blood of Jesus before eating or before being transplanted.

    1 Timothy 4:4–5 says, *"For every creature of God is good, and nothing to be refused, if it be received with thanksgiving: For it is sanctified by the word of God and prayer."*

13. Places – Places for cult worship, nightclubs, beaches, stripper events, hotels, and other meeting places/cities may have been dedicated to perversion such that the seeds of sexual perversion are easily sown in a person's life when they visit such places. Likewise, places sanctified by prayer and by the blood of Jesus will also sow godly seeds to those that visit them.

    Jeremiah 29:7 says, *"And seek the peace of the city whither I have caused you to be carried away captives, and pray unto the LORD for it: for in the peace thereof shall ye have peace."*

14. Dress fashion – Wearing garments or using objects that represent such perversion can also sow seeds of sexual perversion. Sharing garments or sexual objects/enhancers with sexually perverted people can also have the same effect. Some of these can be undergarments manufactured to enhance perversions and, therefore, plant evil seeds into your life. It is advisable to pray and sanctify all garments with the blood of Jesus before wearing or using them so that they will carry the presence of God.

    Acts 19:11–12 says, *"And God wrought special miracles by the hands of Paul: so that from his body were brought unto the sick handkerchiefs or aprons, and the diseases departed from them, and the evil spirits went out of them."*

15. Sexual contact – Getting sexually involved with people carrying such perversions can cause seeds of sexual perversion to be sown in your life. Activities including mutual masturbations, touching someone's private parts, romantic massages, watching live sex, kissing, and other forms of sexual contact will transfer spirits of sexual perversion to your life.

    1 Corinthians 6:16 says, *"What? know ye not that he which is joined to an harlot is one body? for two, says he, shall be one flesh."*

16. Reminisce – Seeds of sexual perversions can also be stirred up by reminiscing about things or previous scenes of sexual perversions. When you find yourself at this point, you need to cleanse your mind immediately to destroy these seeds with the blood of Jesus. Thereafter, ask the spirit of God to sow seeds of purity by reading God's word daily.

    2 Peter 3:1 says, *"This second epistle, beloved, I now write unto you; in both which I stir up your pure minds by way of remembrance."*

17. Cursing – A curse spoken by anyone, especially by someone with authority over you, can cause seeds of sexual perversion to be sown in your life. Your parent or guardian, spiritual leader, employer, witches, and anybody you may have hurt somehow can speak curse words (spells) and sow seeds of sexual perversion in your life. A curse will have an impact on you for a reason which has to be dealt with before it is removed. Such reasons are usually due to unrighteousness.

    Proverbs 26:2 says, *"As the bird by wandering, as the swallow by flying, so the curse causeless shall not come."* Righteousness will cancel the manifestation of a curse.

    In conclusion, when such seeds are sown in your life, they will eventually grow and bear fruit. However, you do not need to wait for the fruits to manifest in your life. You have to pray against them. It does not matter how long it takes for the seeds in the ground to grow. They will wait for a scent of water (opportune moment) to blossom.

Job 14:7–9 says, *"For there is hope of a tree, if it be cut down, that it will sprout again, and that the tender branch thereof will not cease. Though the root thereof wax old in the earth, and the stock thereof die in the ground; Yet through the scent of water it will bud, and bring forth boughs like a plant."* Many people have ever been delivered from sexual perversion but because of allowing these seeds to be sown, they find themselves rejuvenating the lifestyle again.

These seeds can be destroyed before they grow, and the roots can be removed by the power in the blood of Jesus.

Matthew 15:13 says, *"But he answered and said, Every plant, which my heavenly Father hath not planted, shall be rooted up."*

Prayer

Father, in the name of Jesus, I repent all seeds of sexual perversion sown in my life. Lord, I destroy them with the blood of Jesus.

I uproot all evil that has manifested from such seeds in the name of Jesus.

Lord, let the seeds of the kingdom of God be sown in my life to bear good fruit. In Jesus's mighty name. Amen

15

Do You Trust Them?

It took me a long time to understand that every ministry is called and gifted differently according to the needs of the people. I originally believed that all my spiritual needs will be met by the church I attended.

1 Corinthians 12:8–11 says, *"For to one is given by the Spirit the word of wisdom; to another the word of knowledge by the same Spirit; To another faith by the same Spirit; to another the gifts of healing by the same Spirit; To another the working of miracles; to another prophecy; to another discerning of spirits; to another divers kinds of tongues; to another the interpretation of tongues: But all these works that one and the selfsame Spirit, dividing to every man severally as he will."*

Lack of knowledge kept me in bondage for a long time because I did not know that I needed to seek deliverance from homosexuality. Many people, including familiar preachers, were indignant because of their own lack of understanding of spiritual gift giving. The spirit of sexual perversion takes advantage of this discord to keep the victims from receiving their deliverance.

The spirit of perversion caused the Pharisees to accuse Jesus of applying demonic power to do deliverance. The objective was to cause those people who are controlled by demons not to seek help from Jesus, who had the gift of God to set them free. Matthew

12:22–24, 28 says, *"Then was brought unto him one possessed with a devil, blind, and dumb: and he healed him, insomuch that the blind and dumb both spoke and saw. And all the people were amazed, and said, Is not this the son of David? But when the Pharisees heard it, they said, This fellow doth not cast out devils, but by Beelzebub the prince of the devils. But if I cast out devils by the Spirit of God, then the kingdom of God is come unto you."*

This spirit also causes its potential victims to develop a level of trust in places or people it plans to use in launching an attack. The Levite thought that spending a night with his own brethren will be safer than with the Jebusites (nonbelievers). He did not know that this spirit had already planned to use his own brethren to seduce or force him into sexual perversion. Judges 19:11–13, 22 says, *"And when they were by Jebus, the day was far spent; and the servant said unto his master, Come, I pray thee, and let us turn in into this city of the Jebusites, and lodge in it. And his master said unto him, we will not turn aside hither into the city of a stranger, which is not of the children of Israel; we will pass over to Gibeah. And he said unto his servant, Come, and let us draw near to one of these places to lodge all night, in Gibeah. Now as they were making their hearts merry, behold, the men of the city, certain sons of Belial, beset the house round about, and beat at the door, and spoke to the master of the house, the old man, saying, Bring forth the man that came into your house, that we may know [have sexual relations with] him."*

This spirit will attack you through those close to you, including relatives and friends, to fulfil its plan without much hindrance. Many people have been introduced to perverted sexual lifestyles by people they trusted (like uncles, cousins, spiritual leaders, instructors, sponsors, idols, counselors), but Jeremiah 9:4–5 says, *"Take you heed every one of his neighbor, and trust you not in any brother: for every brother will utterly supplant, and every neighbor will walk with slanders. And they will deceive everyone his neighbor, and will not speak the truth: they have taught their tongue to speak lies, and weary themselves to commit iniquity."*

I no longer judge people from what I see or hear. Those we think are dangerous may be innocent and vice versa. Isaiah 11:2–3 says, *"And the spirit of the LORD shall rest upon him, the spirit of wisdom and understanding, the spirit of counsel and might, the spirit of knowledge and of the fear of the LORD; And shall make him of quick understanding in the fear of the LORD: and he shall not judge after the sight of his eyes, neither reprove after the hearing of his ears."* It is therefore important to inquire from the Lord regarding the people in your life and about any place of worship to avoid traps set up to victimize you.

I struggled with homosexuality for almost fifteen years before the Lord spoke to me about where I needed to go for deliverance. The place he told me to go to was accused of being a false church, but I chose to trust God than people's words, and when I obeyed, behold, I was made whole.

Isaiah 30:1–3 says, *"Woe to the rebellious children, says the LORD, that take counsel, but not of me; and that cover with a covering, but not of my spirit, that they may add sin to sin."*

Exodus 23:1–2 says, *"Thou shalt not raise a false report: put not thine hand with the wicked to be an unrighteous witness. Thou shalt not follow a multitude to do evil; neither shalt thou speak in a cause to decline after many to wrest judgment."* Here we are warned never to follow a great number of people who are doing or supporting evil and in this case sexual perversion.

Prayer

Father, in the name of Jesus, I repent the many times I trusted people instead of inquiring from you.

I am sorry for speaking against ministries and people without any knowledge, which has caused me to stay in bondage.

Lord, I ask you to cleanse me of all deception with the blood of Jesus and guide me to the right person or ministry you have gifted for my deliverance in Jesus's mighty name. Amen.

16

The Undercover Boss

The spirit of sexual perversion desires full control of the victim's life and will not tolerate being ignored or described as a bad spirit. It will identify itself in the victim's life as an orientation or as being different. I used to describe myself as someone who struggled with pornography, masturbation or simply as a person of a different sexual orientation. These excuses reduced my guilt for the lifestyle, yet within me, I really knew there was something wrong with my life but could not explain exactly what it was. I appreciated those who approached me with some form of explanation concerning my lifestyle without condemning me.

The spirit of perversion is currently spreading at a fast pace in the lives of innocent people who listen to it's deceptive agents in the form of researchers, activists, medical personnel, and preachers who speak contrary to the truth of the word of God. Victims easily believe without resistance from their consciousness.

1 Timothy 4:1–2 says, *"Now the Spirit speaks expressly, that in the latter times some shall depart from the faith, giving heed to seducing spirits, and doctrines of devils; Speaking lies in hypocrisy; having their conscience seared with a hot iron."* This is evident today where we allow our defiled feelings to take control of our minds and suppress the inner truth in our heart.

As we saw previously regarding the Levite who lodged in Gibeah, he did not tell the children of Israel the truth concerning what had happened to him. He knew the men of Benjamin wanted to have sexual relations with him, but instead, he gave them his concubine, whom they forced until she passed out.

Judges 20:4–5 says, *"And the Levite, the husband of the woman that was slain, answered and said, I came into Gibeah that belongs to Benjamin, I and my concubine, to lodge. And the men of Gibeah rose against me, and beset the house round about upon me by night, and thought to have slain me: and my concubine have they forced, that she is dead."*

This spirit did not allow the Levite to describe it as a homosexual attack in his life but, rather, a homicide. Many homosexuals I have met told me that they were molested when they were young, yet most times, that's not the truth. In reality, they agreed and gave in to the seduction when opportunity knocked on their door but that the spirit can't allow them to disgrace it. Nahum 3:4–5 says, *"Because of the multitude of the whoredoms of the well-favored harlot, the mistress of witchcrafts, that sells nations through her whoredoms, and families through her witchcrafts. Behold, I am against thee, saith the Lord of hosts; and I will discover thy skirts upon thy face, and I will shew the nations thy nakedness, and the kingdoms thy shame."* God has promised to open up the secrets of this well-favored harlot (sexual perversion spirit) so that nations will know its ways.

I recall one time I approached a man of God for prayer and told him that my problem was masturbation instead of telling him the truth that I was struggling with sexual perversion in the form of homosexuality. In addition, there was a time I was dating a girl I wanted to marry, and she found gay pornography in my phone. I dismissed her concerns and told her that I just used the material for masturbation, yet the truth was that I was gay.

Proverbs 28:13 says, *"He that covers his sins shall not prosper: but whoso confesses and forsakes them shall have mercy."* God is opposed to covering up your sins and promises mercy to those who confess and forsake them.

There was also a time I had to share a bed with a fellow minister due to shortage of resources. One day, in the middle of the night, I reached out and touched his private parts. This woke him up, and he was very upset about what I had done. But I told him that it was only a mistake, and he also disregarded it.

Deuteronomy 13:6–8 says, *"If thy brother, the son of thy mother, or thy son, or thy daughter, or the wife of thy bosom, or thy friend, which is as thine own soul, entice thee secretly, saying, Let us go and serve other gods, which thou hast not known, thou, nor thy fathers; Namely, of the gods of the people which are round about you, nigh unto thee, or far off from thee, from the one end of the earth even unto the other end of the earth; Thou shalt not consent unto him, nor hearken unto him; neither shall thine eye pity him, neither shalt thou spare, neither shalt thou conceal him."*

God commands us not to give in to sexual enticements whether it is from a relative, friend, or leader. That we should never conceal what they did to us but reveal it to someone with the ability to be confidential and can also help the victim receive deliverance.

1 Corinthians 6:1–2 says, *"Dare any of you, having a matter against another, go to law before the unjust, and not before the saints? Do you not know that the saints shall judge the world? And if the world shall be judged by you, are you unworthy to judge the smallest matters?"*

It is advisable that such matters are handled privately to avoid shaming the victim. It is also suitable to publicly share your story after deliverance as a testimony of what God has done with the intention of forsaking it and never turning back. Speaking publicly about another person's sexual perversion is disobedience to God's word, and it may bear consequences that may include rejection and persecution.

Colossians 3:13 says, *"Forbearing one another, and forgiving one another, if any man have a quarrel against any: even as Christ forgave you, so also do ye."* We are requested to keep sexual perversion issues about others secret from the public and forgive them who have taken advantage of us. We can only talk about it with confidentiality and only for the purposes of deliverance and not to humiliate the culprits in public.

Matthew 18:15–17 says, *"Moreover if your brother shall trespass against you, go and tell him his fault between you and him alone: if he shall hear you, you have gained your brother. But if he will not hear you, then take with you one or two more, that in the mouth of two or three witnesses every word may be established. And if he shall neglect to hear them, tell it unto the church: but if he neglects to hear the church, let him be unto you as a heathen man and a publican."*

Prayer

Father, in the name of Jesus, I repent for not forgiving those who seduced me into committing sexual perversion. Forgive me, Lord, and cleanse me of all revenge, anger, bitterness, unforgiveness, and pain with the blood of Jesus.

Lord, give me a heart to forgive. Fill me with joy and peace in my heart so that I will not revenge against anyone. Give me your spirit to guide me on how to get my deliverance and to help others find their deliverance in Jesus's name. Amen.

17

Treats for Influential People

The spirit of sexual perversion has an inclination toward leaders or people of influence as a channel to access the masses who look up to them for counsel, guidance, and support. These include adults in a family unit, media icons, educational leaders, spiritual leaders, economical leaders, political leaders, music idols, sports icons, and many others.

This spirit intensified its work in me when I became a leader in the church because it knew that I was going to have young people under my leadership. I received a lot of favor, and many youths desired to be just like me. These young people took great interest in how I dressed, walked, and talked. They also wanted to hung around me whenever I traveled out of town. A good number of my subordinates adopted my hobbies, including my homosexual lifestyle, either because they wanted acceptance and favors from me or they probably thought that whatever I did as their leader was the right thing.

I caution every leader in any capacity to be aware of this spirit in their own lives and other leaders in their jurisdiction.

1 Chronicles 14:8 says, *"And when the Philistines heard that David was anointed king over all Israel, all the Philistines went up to seek David. And David heard of it, and went out against them."*

The Philistines only sought after David when they learned that he had become a leader. Thank God that David prepared an attack against them when he also learned that they were after him. This is what successful leaders are supposed to do against the spirit of sexual perversion.

God knows that this spirit will attack leaders, that is why he is very strict on who qualifies to be a leader at any level of society, especially in His church.

Deuteronomy 17:15–16 says, *"You shall in any wise set him king over thee, whom the LORD thy God shall choose: one from among thy brethren shall you set king over thee: you may not set a stranger [someone not tried and proven] over thee, which is not thy brother [someone without godly character]. But he shall not multiply horses to himself, nor cause the people to return to Egypt [perverted lifestyles], to the end that he should multiply horses: forasmuch as the LORD hath said unto you, you shall henceforth return no more that way."*

A brother is someone you know publicly and in private who must be chosen by the Lord. God anoints those he chooses, and his anointing confers victory when one is attacked. A leader must be able to overcome the enemy's attacks. Zechariah 13:7 says, *"Awake, O sword, against my shepherd, and against the man that is my fellow, says the LORD of hosts: smite the shepherd, and the sheep shall be scattered: and I will turn mine hand upon the little ones."*

When a leader is overcome by the spirit of sexual perversion, that spirit will be transferred to the subordinates (whether little ones or old ones). They will be imparted with his lifestyle.

1 Kings 15:30 says, *"Because of the sins of Jeroboam which he sinned, and which he made Israel sin, by his provocation wherewith he provoked the LORD God of Israel to anger."* King Jeroboam lived a perverted lifestyle and inspired the entire nation to live like he did, which provoked the anger of the Lord. Many leaders committing sexual perversion fail to acknowledge that their inspiration affects the people they lead. They also tend to give out favors and promotions to those who condone their lifestyle thereby converting the uninformed.

The Lord warns in 1 Timothy 5:2 and 24, *"Lay hands suddenly on no man (separating them for leadership), neither be partaker of other men's sins: keep thyself pure. Some men's sins are open beforehand, going before to judgment; and some men they follow after."*

It is very hard to perceive the spirit of sexual perversion in a leader. That's why it is very important to pray for our leaders and also ask God to reveal to us their struggles. God will do it if your intentions are to help them to be free and not to shame them.

1 Timothy 2:1–2 says, *"I exhort therefore, that, first of all, supplications, prayers, intercessions, and giving of thanks, be made for all men; For kings, and for all that are in authority; that we may lead a quiet and peaceable life in all godliness and honesty."*

Psalm 125:3 says, *"For the rod [leadership ♡♧] of the wicked shall not rest upon the lot [society] of the righteous; lest the righteous put forth their hands unto iniquity."*

Proverbs 29:2 says, *"When the righteous are in authority, the people rejoice: but when the wicked bears rule, the people mourn."*

We have heard a lot of complaints from young people being molested by their leaders. Whenever anyone is molested, they become subjected to the control of this spirit spiritually and morally. This effect will grow as seeds and, in turn, the molested individual will begin to molest others unless they are delivered by the power of God, which is through the blood of Jesus Christ.

Prayer

Father, in the name of Jesus, I repent for not praying for my leaders but just criticize them. Lord, I ask you to give me a heart to stand in the gap on behalf of my leaders.

Lord, I ask you to open my eyes as a leader to see the battle around me so that I may fight accordingly. I repent having caused your people to go astray when they followed in my footsteps and sinned against you.

Wash away everything in me that has provoked your anger with the blood of Jesus. I dedicate my life and those under my leadership to the blood of Jesus. Please deliver us from perverted lifestyles and cause us to serve you.

Lord, show me a way out of all perversions and guide me with your spirit to lead many toward deliverance. In Jesus's mighty name. Amen.

18

Anointed Dead Body

Scripture is very clear about sexual perversion, and certainly, it was not God's will for me. It is ironic that I was still anointed to preach and pray for the sick despite the filthy lifestyle I lead. On one occasion, I received a two-hour notice to preach. I was having a sexual affair with a certain guy when the phone rang. I did not have time to pray nor prepare, but when I stood on the pulpit, God's anointing upon me was heavy. We witnessed healing, and people received miracles in the name of the Lord. We continued to witness God's goodness on numerous occasions, and I was rather astonished. It was after I received my deliverance that I understood what had happened to me when the Lord explained to me the mystery of his anointing.

Leviticus 20:13 says, *"If a man also lie with a man, as he lies with a woman, both of them have committed an abomination: they shall surely be put to death; their blood shall be upon them."* When I slept with my fellow guys, I never died as this scripture claims, and I was convinced that scripture is outdated.

The same thing happened to Adam and Eve when the devil convinced them that they would not surely die as the Lord had said. That's why they disobeyed God and ate of the fruit; their death was a spiritual death. The devil kept whispering in my mind that "God would have killed you immediately if he hated your lifestyle," yet the truth is that I had suffered a spiritual death.

Sin causes spiritual death, which means a separation from the presence of God, or the absence of God's manifestation in one's life. Moses insisted that God should go with them into the Promised Land because he knew the difference between his presence and an angel (anointing/charisma).

Exodus 33:2–3, 15–16 says, *"And I will send an angel before thee; and I will drive out the Canaanite, the Amorite, and the Hittite, and the Perizzite, the Hivite, and the Jebusite: Unto a land flowing with milk and honey: for I will not go up in the midst of thee; for thou art a stiff necked people: lest I consume thee in the way. And he said unto him; if thy presence goes not with me, carry us not up hence. For wherein shall it be known here that I and thy people have found grace in thy sight? Is it not in that you go with us? So shall we be separated, I and thy people, from all the people that are upon the face of the earth."*

This scripture tells us that one can be in sin (with a stiff neck) and have the anointing (angel) to perform miracles, drive out enemies, and also bring to pass the promises of God but not the presence of God. Moses knew that God's presence will keep them safe, make them special and keep them from perverted lifestyles of the nations they were to possess.

When Jesus was on the cross, for a moment, he felt the absence of God due to the sin of the world he was carrying, which was proof that the real presence of God cannot dwell where sin is.

Mathew 27:46 says, *"And about the ninth hour Jesus cried with a loud voice, saying, Eli, Eli, lama sabachthani? That is to say, My God, my God, why hast thou forsaken me?"*

Even in death, Prophet Elisha's remains retained God's anointing. 2 Kings 13:21 says, *"And it came to pass, as they were burying a man, that, behold, they spied a band of men; and they cast the man into the sepulcher of Elisha: and when the man was let down, and touched the bones of Elisha, he revived, and stood up on his feet."*

A person may sin and die spiritually but maintain the anointing to cause a revival in another person's life and circumstances. The primary purpose of God's anointing is to meet the needs of his people, and God will chose whomever he pleases to fulfil his purpose as he did for the children of Israel.

Isaiah 45:1 and 4 says, *"Thus says the LORD to his anointed, to Cyrus, whose right hand I have Holden, to subdue nations before him; and I will loose the loins of kings, to open before him the two leaved gates; and the gates shall not be shut; For Jacob my servant's sake and Israel mine elect, I have even called thee by thy name: I have surnamed thee, though thou hast not known me."*

Cyrus was chosen and anointed to be king when he did not know God. This confirms that God's anointing is always for a purpose of meeting the needs of his people, not necessarily a proof that you know him or carry his presence within you.

Scripture shows us how the spirit of the Lord operates in our lives. Matthew 3:15 says, *"And Jesus answering said unto him, suffer it to be so now: for thus it becomes us to fulfill all righteousness. Then he suffered him."*

Luke 4:1 says, *"And Jesus being full of the Holy Ghost returned from Jordan, and was led by the Spirit into the wilderness."* Jesus was full of the Holy Ghost after He fulfilled all righteousness.

The spirit led Jesus into the wilderness to be tempted of the devil, and the spirit of the Lord also came upon Jesus and anointed him for ministry. Luke 4:18 says, *"The Spirit of the Lord is upon me, because he hath anointed me to preach the gospel to the poor; he hath sent me to heal the brokenhearted, to preach deliverance to the captives, and recovering of sight to the blind, to set at liberty them that are bruised."*

Each measure of the spirit of God that Jesus received served a different purpose in His life.

Measures of the Spirit in Jesus's Life

The spirit within: This is the measure of the spirit received when one truly repents and receives the righteousness of God. He is the seal of redemption, and he is God's presence in that believer. Ephesians 4:30 says, *"And grieve not the Holy Spirit of God, whereby ye are sealed unto the day of redemption."*

This spirit can be grieved and can also be taken away from a believer when they sin and don't truly repent. This is the spirit who left King Saul when he sinned and failed to truly repent.

1 Samuel 16:14 says, *"But the Spirit of the LORD departed from Saul, and an evil spirit from the LORD troubled him."*

This is the same spirit who king David cried out for, not to be taken away from him when he sinned. Psalm 51:11 says, *"Cast me not away from thy presence; and take not thy Holy Spirit from me."* Repeated sin and lack of true repentance will break the seal of redemption and cause the spirit of God to depart from you whereby losing your connection to God.

Luke 13:25–27 says, *"When once the master of the house is risen up, and hath shut to the door, and ye begin to stand without, and to knock at the door, saying, Lord, Lord, open unto us; and he shall answer and say unto you, I know you not whence ye are: Then shall ye begin to say, We have eaten and drunk in thy presence, and thou hast taught in our streets. But he shall say, I tell you, I know you not whence ye are; depart from me, all ye workers of iniquity."*

The spirit with us: This is the measure of the spirit of God who guides and leads us in different ways in our daily lives. He can prompt those who do not know God into doing something they would not have intended to do. He can also change your plans to save you from harm. People usually speak of him as "Something told me," usually after avoiding some mishap. This is the spirit who protects us from the enemy's plots even before we come to know the Lord, knowing that one day we will repent and serve the Lord. Genesis 41:25, 29–30 says, *"And Joseph said unto Pharaoh, The dream of Pharaoh is one: God hath shewed Pharaoh what he is about to do. Behold, there come seven years of great plenty throughout all the land of Egypt: And there shall arise after them seven years of famine; and all the plenty shall be forgotten in the land of Egypt; and the famine shall consume the land."*

This is the spirit who speaks to us in dreams with warnings or leads that tell us to what to do. He did this to many kings and to the wise men that came to see Jesus.

Mathew 2:12 says, *"And being warned of God in a dream that they should not return to Herod, they departed into their own country another way."*

The spirit upon us: This is the spirit that anoints people with talents for the work of the kingdom of God here on earth as purposed by God. Unfortunately, many people use these talents (gifts) to serve Satan or their own will, knowingly or unknowingly.

Romans 11:29 says, *"For the gifts and calling of God are without repentance."*

God doesn't take away his gifts and calling, but everyone will give accountability of how they were used on Judgment Day.

Mathew 25:14–15, 19, 30 says, *"For the kingdom of heaven is as a man traveling into a far country, who called his own servants, and delivered unto them his goods. And unto one he gave five talents, to another two, and to another one; to every man according to his several ability; and straightway took his journey. After a long time the lord of those servants cometh, and reckoned with them. And he said cast ye the unprofitable servant into outer darkness: there shall be weeping and gnashing of teeth."*

Prayer

Father, in the name of Jesus, I ask you to open my eyes to understand the difference between your presence and anointing.

Lord, forgive me of all sin that has caused your presence to shift from me and revive me from spiritual death by the blood of Jesus.

Restore your spirit within me as your seal of ownership. Guide me by your spirit on what to do with the talents you have entrusted me with. Let your anointing be upon me to establish your kingdom on earth in Jesus's mighty name. Amen.

19

My Worship

The concept of godly worship began with Abraham, and he teaches us what real worship is. Worship involves three main parts: an altar, a sacrifice, and a priest who renders the worship. Acceptable worship is conducted according to the laws of whom worship is due.

Genesis 22:5, 9, 12–13 says, *"And Abraham said unto his young men, Abide ye here with the ass; and I and the boy will go yonder and worship, and come again to you. And they came to the place which God had told him of; and Abraham built an altar there, and laid the wood in order, and bound Isaac his son, and laid him on the altar upon the wood. And the angel of the Lord said, Lay not your hand upon the boy, neither do you anything unto him: for now I know that you fear God, seeing you have not withheld your son, your only son from me. And Abraham lifted up his eyes, and looked, and behold behind him a ram caught in a thicket by his horns: and Abraham went and took the ram, and offered him up for a burnt offering in the stead of his son."*

Godly worship involves separating yourself from anyone or anything that does not agree with the principles of the Lord like Abraham did. It involves building an altar (place of worship), a sacrifice (God no longer requires killing of creatures as sacrifice), and a priest rendering the worship. Many people today go to places of worship and are deceived that they are worshiping the God of heaven yet hating his principles.

Mark 7:6–7 says, *"He answered and said unto them, Well hath Esaias prophesied of you hypocrites, as it is written, This people honor me with their lips, but their heart is far from me. Howbeit in vain do they worship me, teaching for doctrines the commandments of men."* If what is being taught where you worship is not what God commands in his word then that worship is in vain.

John 4:23 says, *"Jesus said but the hour comes, and now is, when the true worshippers shall worship the Father in spirit and in truth: for the Father seeks such to worship him."* This implies that true worship is about what is in your spirit or heart, not what you speak of or teach or where you go to worship. Going to a right place of worship yet with a defiled heart or spirit will not also constitute true worship. All factors of worship are equally important.

There was a time when I could not close my eyes to meditate on the Lord during a worship service due to the pornographic images that constantly played in my mind. This rendered my worship to Satan because the contents of my mind and soul were not an acceptable sacrifice to God.

Romans 12:1–2 says, *"I beseech you therefore, brethren, by the mercies of God, that ye present your bodies a living sacrifice, holy, acceptable unto God, which is your reasonable service. And be not conformed to this world: but be ye transformed by the renewing of your mind, that ye may prove what is that good, and acceptable, and perfect, will of God."*

The thoughts of our heart and what we do with our bodies, including our lifestyle, become a form of worship to the one we submit it to. The God of heaven requires us to keep our bodies undefiled (holy) and our minds pure.

Exodus 34:13–14 says, *"But you shall destroy their altars, break their images, and cut down their groves: For you shall worship no other god: for the LORD, whose name is Jealous, is a jealous God."*

The God of heaven requires us to destroy all altars of other gods (the spirit of sexual perversion is a god) in our lives. We need to clean our minds of their images to stop their control in our lives. It is only with a clean mind that we can offer acceptable worship to God, for he is a jealous God.

Romans 1:24–25 says, *"Wherefore God also gave them up to uncleanness through the lusts of their own hearts, to dishonor their own bodies between themselves: Who changed the truth of God into a lie, and worshipped and served the creature more than the Creator, who is blessed forever. Amen."* So we realize that dishonoring our bodies through sexual perversion is a worship rendered to the creature (Satan), not the creator.

When we consider the concept of the altar, sacrifice, and priest, I realized that my sexual involvement with another man was literally a form of worship service. Notably, I was the priest, the bed represented the altar, and my mate became a living sacrifice being offered to the god of sexual perversion.

1 Kings 14:22–24 says, *"And Judah did evil in the sight of the LORD, and they provoked Him to jealousy with their sins which they had committed, above all that their fathers had done. For they also built them high places, and images, and groves, on every high hill, and under every green tree. And there were also sodomites in the land: and they did according to all the abominations of the nations which the LORD cast out before the children of Israel."*

The God of heaven is concerned about who we go to bed with and what we do in that worship service.

Hebrews 13:4 says, *"Marriage is honorable in all, and the bed undefiled: but whoremongers and adulterers God will judge."*

According to God's principles, the person you go to bed with for a sexual affair must be one individual, married to you, of the opposite sex, and the same individual all the time. The worship (making of love) should not be against nature.

Romans 1:26–27 says, *"For this cause God gave them up unto vile affections: for even their women did change the natural use into that which is against nature: And likewise also the men, leaving the natural use of the woman, burned in their lust one toward another;*

men with men working that which is unseemly, and receiving in themselves that recompence of their error which was meet."

Prayer

Father, in the name of Jesus, I repent of all worship I have rendered to the god of sexual perversion. Please forgive me, Lord, and wash me from idolatry with the blood of Jesus Christ.

Lord, separate me from anyone and anything that contributes to idol worship in my life through the blood of Jesus. Connect me to people who will help me practice true biblical worship to you. In Jesus's mighty name. Amen.

20

Sodom—The garden of the lord

The city of Sodom looked like the garden of the Lord in Lot's perception. It appeared to be well watered and appeared more prosperous than the other cities. Lot, therefore, chose Sodom for his habitation being deceived by its current state (physical status), yet its future (spiritual status) was not certain.

Before my deliverance, I used to get angry whenever anyone talked about Sodom and Gomorrah, wondering whether they had nothing to talk about or whether homosexuality was the only sin in Sodom.

Genesis 13:10–12 says, *"And Lot lifted up his eyes, and beheld all the plain of Jordan, that it was well watered everywhere, before the LORD destroyed Sodom and Gomorrah, even as the garden of the LORD, like the land of Egypt, as thou comes unto Zoar. Then Lot chose him all the plain of Jordan; and Lot journeyed east: and they separated themselves the one from the other. Abram dwelled in the land of Canaan, and Lot dwelled in the cities of the plain, and pitched his tent toward Sodom."*

My mind encountered similar deception as that of Lot when I considered how prosperous the people controlled by the spirit of sexual perversion were. They were successful in music, sports, business, politics, the film industry, in education, and even appeared so in the religious world. I, therefore, concluded that the blessing of God was upon them.

However, Jesus says in Revelation 3:17–19, *"Because you say, I am rich, and increased with goods, and have need of nothing; and know not that you are wretched, and miserable, and poor, and blind, and naked: I counsel you to buy of me gold tried in the fire, that you may be rich; and white raiment, that you may be clothed, and that the shame of your nakedness does not appear; and anoint your eyes with eye salve, that you may see. As many as I love, I rebuke and chasten: be zealous therefore, and repent."*

This is when I realized that this spirit strategically attacks influential people for the purpose of using them to attract masses to its control as they crave for temporary successes.

Scripture warns us in Psalm 92:7: *"When the wicked spring as the grass, and when all the workers of iniquity do flourish; it is because they shall be destroyed forever."*

As it is with many people, scripture is perceived as rather inapplicable or untrue; however, the truth soon manifests regardless of one's belief.

After my deliverance, the Lord asked me to speak to my ex-sexual partners about repenting and turning to the Lord. In particular, there was a young man called Ronnie, who had become popular and prosperous in his career as a porn star. The Lord told me that his days were numbered and he needed to repent. I obeyed what the Lord said to me and went out to look for Ronnie. He looked healthy and was very confident in the future of his career. I told Ronnie what the Lord had told me about him, but he disregarded my words as folly and probably thought that I just needed something from him. I had to leave shortly thereafter.

About six months later, I was told that, for some reason, Ronnie fainted and died on his way to the hospital. I was so sorry to hear about his sudden death, but this was a result of rejecting the word of God. Ronnie made his ultimate choice. Media, which is a tool for the spirit of sexual perversion, does never show the end of these people we highly regard as successful through their sexually perverted lifestyle, but from research, most of them have a miserable end.

Some have died in pain because of incurable sexually transmitted infections, being shot at in fights for being unfaithful to their partners, committing suicide after failing to get peace in their transgender status, being offered as ritual sacrifices for perverted business successes, accidents during sexual orgies, drug overdose to maintain sexual libido, or passing out during forced perversions. Others are living with severe heartbreak due to unfaithfulness, damaged health of the body systems, trauma from past experiences in their careers in sex, loss of families due to homophobia, regret for irreversible decisions, and many more.

Psalm 73:1–6, 16–19 says, *"Truly God is good to Israel, even to such as are of a clean heart. But as for me, my feet were almost gone; my steps had well nigh slipped. For I was envious at the foolish, when I saw the prosperity of the wicked. For there are no bands in their death: but their strength is firm. They are not in trouble as other men; neither are they plagued like other men. Therefore pride compasses them about as a chain; violence covers them as a garment. When I thought to know this, it was too painful for me; Until I went into the sanctuary of God; then understood I their end. Surely thou didst set them in slippery places: thou casts them down into destruction."*

I have come across tons of false teachings from the different corners of the world that are designed by Satan to destroy many innocent lives by means of making evil look good and good look evil. God condemns such teachings, and both those who produce them and they that listen to them are destined for destruction as per the warning of scripture.

Jude 1:4–5, 7 says, *"For there are certain men crept in unawares, who were before of old ordained to this condemnation, ungodly men, turning the grace of our God into lasciviousness [life without restraints], and denying the only Lord God, and our Lord Jesus Christ. I will therefore put you in remembrance, though ye once knew this, how that the Lord, having saved the people out of the land of Egypt, afterward destroyed them that believed not. Even as Sodom and Gomorrah, and the cities about them in like manner, giving themselves over to fornication, and going after strange flesh, are set forth for an example, suffering the vengeance of eternal fire."*

These false teachings include ideas like Jesus was gay because all his twelve disciples were men and there was one who always leaned on Jesus's bosom. The scripture is clear: the disciple was leaning (not sleeping) on Jesus's chest in the presence of all other disciples and in only one occasion of the Last Supper, meaning there was nothing sexual. This disciple was John, and he was the youngest of all the disciples. Jesus had a father/son relationship with him and loved him as a father would love his youngest child with extra special care. He also requested his mother to take care of John after his departure.

Jesus compared the calamity that befell those who dwelt in the city of Sodom to what will happen on the day of Judgment.

Luke 17:28–30 says, *"Likewise also as it was in the days of Lot; they did eat, they drank, they bought, they sold, they planted, and they built; But the same day that Lot went out of Sodom it rained fire and brimstone from heaven, and destroyed them all. Even thus shall it be in the day when the Son of man is revealed."*

When Jesus recognizes that it was appropriate for Sodom to be punished with fire and brimstone further proves that Jesus was not gay. A gay person cannot truly condemn homosexuality.

Jesus was tempted in all ways as we are tempted today, but he did not give in to sin, and he expects the same with us.

Hebrews 4:15 says, *"For we have not an high priest which cannot be touched with the feeling of our infirmities; but was in all points tempted like as we are, yet without sin."* Therefore, this teaching about Jesus being gay is a total lie.

The other false teaching is that homosexuals will inherit the kingdom of God without repenting and turning away from their lifestyle.

According to scripture, 1 Corinthians 6:9–10 says, *"Know ye not that the unrighteous shall not inherit the kingdom of God? Be not deceived: neither fornicators, nor idolaters, nor adulterers, nor effeminate, nor abusers of themselves with mankind [homosexuals],*

Nor thieves, nor covetous, nor drunkards, nor revilers, nor extortionists, shall inherit the kingdom of God."

The categories of people who cannot inherit the kingdom of God according to scripture includes homosexuals and many other sins.

Deuteronomy 23:17–18 says, *"There shall be no whore [prostitute] of the daughters of Israel, nor a sodomite [homosexual] of the sons of Israel. Thou shall not bring the hire of a whore, or the price of a dog [homosexual], into the house of the LORD thy God for any vow: for even both these are abominations unto the LORD thy God."* This means that one cannot be a true son of Israel (Son of God) and a homosexual at the same time; one cancels out the other. Even wages gotten through sexual perversion services are unacceptable to the Lord for an offering.

To confirm the above scripture, the Lord continues to say in Leviticus 18:22–24, *"Thou shall not lie with mankind, as with womankind: it is abomination. Neither shall you lie with any beast to defile thyself therewith: neither shall any woman stand before a beast to lie down thereto: it is confusion. Defile not ye yourselves in any of these things: for in all these the nations are defiled which I cast out before you."*

Another false teaching supports the coming out of the closet to announce to the public that you are either gay or a lesbian, but Isaiah 3:8–9 says, *"For Jerusalem is ruined, and Judah is fallen: because their tongue and their doings are against the LORD, to provoke the eyes of His glory. The show (pride parade) of their countenance does witness against them, and they declare their sin as Sodom. They hide it not. Woe unto their soul, for they have rewarded evil unto themselves!"*

Coming out of the closet should be with a purpose of seeking help on how to repent, forsake, and be delivered from the sexual perversion. Proverbs 28:13 says, *"He that covers his sins shall not prosper: but whoso confesses and forsakes them shall have mercy."* So we confess to forsake not confess to be accepted.

The other false teaching was that you are saved by grace, and it doesn't matter what you do with your body in this life. Your salvation is eternal as long as you trusted in Jesus for your redemption. Revelation 14:13 says, *"And I heard a voice from heaven saying unto me, write, blessed are the dead which die in the Lord from henceforth: Yea, says the Spirit, that they may rest from their labors; and their works do follow them."* This reveals that I am blessed if I died, trusting the Lord for my redemption and the works I have done while in my body on earth will follow me.

Revelation 20:12–13 says, *"And I saw the dead, small and great, stand before God; and the books were opened: and another book was opened, which is the book of life: and the dead were judged out of those things which were written in the books, according to their works. And the sea gave up the dead which were in it; and death and hell delivered up the dead which were in them: and they were judged every man according to their works."*

Every man is going to be judged according to his works and not what Jesus did for us. This means that after giving my life to the Lord, He forgives and removes my past evil works and now I have to do good works, which are proof of my repentance.

Luke 3:8 says, *"Bring forth therefore fruits worthy of repentance, and begin not to say within yourselves, We have Abraham to our father: for I say unto you, That God is able of these stones to raise up children unto Abraham."* John the Baptist warned Israel not to be deceived and continue their sin because Abraham was their father. John urged them to bring fruits as proof of their repentance.

Luke 6:46–48 says, *"And why call you me, Lord, Lord, and do not the things which I say? Whosoever comes to me, and hears my sayings and does them, I will show you to whom he is like: He is like a man which built an house, and dug deep, and laid the foundation on a rock: and when the flood arose, the stream beat vehemently upon that house, and could not shake it: for it was founded upon a rock."*

Another false teaching is that there is nothing I can do to make God to love me, but John 14:23–24 says, *"Jesus answered and said unto him, If a man love me, he will keep my words: and my Father will love him, and we will come unto him, and make our abode with him. This implies God would love me if I kept Jesus's words and they together will come and stay with me."*

1 John 2:3–4 says, *"And hereby we do know that we know him, if we keep his commandments. He that says, I know him, and keeps not his commandments, is a liar, and the truth is not in him."*

Prayer

Father, in the name of Jesus, I repent coveting the wicked and wanting to be like them because of their temporary success. Lord, I didn't know that their end is always miserable.

I have been deceived by their outward appearance, and my mind has been defiled by their false teachings, but now I ask you to wash me with the blood of your son, Jesus Christ. Make my garments white and seal me with your Holy Spirit.

Lord, don't allow me to be like Lot who chose Sodom because it looked watered and prosperous but show me the right way to good life and to inherit the kingdom of God in Jesus's mighty name. Amen.

21

The Evening Ride

There is a time and a season for everything under heaven, including the functioning of spiritual beings. God has appointed times and seasons, Satan has also identified himself with that spiritual principle. I realized that the spirit of sexual perversion always had a ride to offer to anyone who responded in the evening hour. I used to get a great urge to have a sexual affair during the evening hours. This spirit intensifies its control mechanism in every person under its control during its peak time, the evening hour.

Isaiah 60:22 says, *"A little one shall become a thousand and a small one a strong nation: I the LORD will hasten it in his time."* God promises to intensify his work at the right time; this can be an appointed hour, day, month or year. According to scripture, Elijah had knowledge about times and seasons that compelled him to wait for the appropriate evening sacrifice hour to prepare God's altar in which he sacrificed and prayed for an answer by fire.

1 Kings 18:29–30 says, *"And it came to pass, when midday was past, and they prophesied until the time of the offering of the evening sacrifice, that there was neither voice, nor any to answer, nor any that regarded. And Elijah said unto all the people, Come near unto me. And all the people came near unto him. And he repaired the altar of the LORD that was broken down."*

There is an appointed day that the Lord ordains for delivering a person, and it will surely happen if that person persists in the presence of God, praying until that appointed time. Isaiah 49:8 says, *"Thus saith the Lord, In an acceptable time have I heard thee, and in a day of salvation have I helped thee: and I will preserve thee, and give thee for a covenant of the people, to establish the earth, to cause to inherit the desolate heritages."*

It took me some time to get total freedom from the spirit of sexual perversion. I was taught the word, I applied it in my life, I repented, and I cancelled all satanic covenants. I asked God what he wanted me to do, and he told me to wait for him as I evangelized inmates in a certain prison. I made a vow to serve him with my story wherever he would open a door for me, I prayed and fasted for others with the same bondage as I had, and I sowed financial seeds until the appointed time of my deliverance came. God visited me in a dream, and he showed me when I was fighting the spirit of sexual perversion in the form of a man, and I killed him. From that day, my desires changed, and I started hating what I had dearly craved for. So it's important to patiently seek God and wait for his acceptable time of deliverance. It may be quick or delayed, depending on what is in your heart or your obedience to the instructions given by God.

Exodus 12:41–42 says, *"And it came to pass at the end of the four hundred and thirty years, even the selfsame day it came to pass, that all the hosts of the LORD went out from the land of Egypt. It is a night to be much observed unto the Lord for bringing them out from the land of Egypt: this is that night of the Lord to be observed of all the children of Israel in their generations."*

Satan has identified himself with the different spiritual times and seasons. You can also focus on the peak times to attack and prevail against such evil spirits with the blood of Jesus. The spirit of death usually intensifies past the midnight hour while the spirit of sexual perversion and drunkenness intensify beginning 5:00 p.m. The spirit of sexual perversion causes weird and lustful thoughts in the minds of its victims during this time. It increases sexual desires and sets traps (seducers) to catch anyone available.

2 Samuel 11:2 says, *"And it came to pass in an evening tide, that*

David arose from off his bed, and walked upon the roof of the king's house: and from the roof he saw a woman washing herself; and the woman was very beautiful to look upon." King David left his bed in the evening time and walked on the rooftop of his house. This was a trap set by the spirit of sexual perversion. David could not resist the beauty of the woman he saw bathing.

I used to walk around the neighborhood (at the park, at the beach, around bars, around dance clubs) in the evening time in search of anyone with a similar interest to hook up with. When I ran out of luck, I would stalk someone taking a shower to satisfy my eyes, or log on to social sites to find a hookup for that night. On other days, I would turn off all sources of sound in my room in order to hear any performance sounds from next-door apartments. This spirit had such a strong grip on me in the nighttime such that I could leave a church night service to go have a sexual affair with a guy and return to service later.

Jeremiah 6:4–5 says, *"Prepare you war against her; arise, and let us go up at noon. Woe unto us! For the day goes away, for the shadows of the evening are stretched out. Arise, and let us go by night, and let us destroy her palaces."* This is a planning meeting for the spirits of sexual perversion arising to attack individuals who have no insight to spiritual timing and seasons.

Genesis 19:4–5 says, *"But before they lay down, the men of the city, even the men of Sodom, compassed the house round, both old and young, all the people from every quarter: And they called unto Lot, and said unto him, where are the men who came in to thee this night? Bring them out unto us, that we may know [have sexual affairs with] them."* Since this spirit usually prepares to attack in the night, it means we should be more watchful at night. This is when you expect it to make its advances through seduction or someone attractive. It is scriptural to counterattack it with prayer during the night, using the blood of Jesus and the word of God. Paul and Silas were arrested and put in bondage by such evil spirits. However, their knowledge of the power of the midnight prayer caused their chains to break loose.

Acts 16:25–26 says, *"And at midnight Paul and Silas prayed, and sang praises unto God: and the prisoners heard them. And suddenly there was a great earthquake, so that the foundations of the prison were shaken: and immediately all the doors were opened, and every one's bands were loosed."*

The children of Israel had been held captive by their taskmasters for four hundred years. God warned them to watch for the midnight hour when he would come to break their captivity.

Exodus 12:12–13, 29 says, *"For I will pass through the land of Egypt this night, and will smite all the firstborn in the land of Egypt, both man and beast; and against all the gods of Egypt I will execute judgment: I am the LORD. And the blood shall be to you for a token upon the houses where ye are: and when I see the blood, I will pass over you, and the plague shall not be upon you to destroy you, when I smite the land of Egypt. And it came to pass, that at midnight the Lord smote all the firstborn in the land of Egypt, from the firstborn of Pharaoh that sat on his throne unto the firstborn of the captive that was in the dungeon; and all the firstborn of cattle."*

Prayer

Father, in the name of Jesus, I repent being ignorant of times and seasons when spiritual beings operate.

I ask you, Lord, to circumcise my heart and my ears to hear your instructions concerning my deliverance. Help me to be obedient so that I may access my acceptable time.

Lord, wash away all blindness from my spirit with the blood of Jesus. Give me your Holy Spirit to strengthen me to wait upon you without growing weary, and that I may prevail against the spirit of sexual perversion. In Jesus's mighty name. Amen.

22

Spirit of Truth

Before the Lord Jesus went back to heaven, He promised us a comforter, also called the spirit of truth, who would help us as we go through life's struggles.

John 16:13–14 says, *"Howbeit when He, the Spirit of truth, is come, He will guide you into all truth: for He shall not speak of himself; but whatsoever He shall hear, that shall He speak: and He will show you things to come. He shall glorify me: for He shall receive of mine, and shall show it unto you."*

Since the spirit of God is the spirit of truth, we conclude that Satan's spirits are of deception. Sexual perversion is from Satan, which makes it a spirit of deception.

John 8:44 says, *"You are of your father the devil, and the lusts of your father you will do. He was a murderer from the beginning, and abode not in the truth, because there is no truth in him. When he speaks a lie, he speaks of his own: for he is a liar, and the father of it."* We can overcome the spirit of sexual perversion by the Spirit of truth who is primarily spoken of in the word of God [the Holy Bible]."

Anything that God has to say about any matter pertaining to our life is found in the scriptures. 2 Peter 1:20–21 says, *"Knowing this first, that no prophecy of the scripture is of any private interpretation. For the prophecy came not in old time by the will of man: but holy men of God spoke as they were moved by the Holy Ghost."*

The spirit of truth inspired holy men of God to write the Lord's counsel in all matters concerning life for generations to come. These scriptures are not to be interpreted for any private benefit but are self-explanatory.

1 Timothy 4:1–2 says, *"Now the Spirit speaks expressly, that in the latter times some shall depart from the faith, giving heed to seducing spirits, and doctrines of devils; Speaking lies in hypocrisy; having their conscience seared with a hot iron."*

I fell prey to the doctrine of devils and was seduced into sexual perversion. I was content as a homosexual because my conscience had been seared with a hot iron to believe that God created me as a homosexual and I did not need to live in denial.

But the spirit of truth in 1 Corinthians 6:9–11 says, *"Know ye not that the unrighteous shall not inherit the kingdom of God? Be not deceived: neither fornicators, nor idolaters, nor adulterers, nor effeminate, nor those that participate in homosexuality, Nor thieves, nor covetous, nor drunkards, nor revilers, nor extortionists, shall inherit the kingdom of God. And such were some of you: but ye are washed, but ye are sanctified, but ye are justified in the name of the Lord Jesus, and by the Spirit of our God."*

So we realize that God from the old times has been delivering people from sexual perversion by washing them, sanctifying them, and justifying them when they believe in the name of Jesus to receive the spirit of truth.

Acts 2:38 says, *"Then Peter said unto them, repent, and be baptized every one of you in the name of Jesus Christ for the remission of sins, and ye shall receive the gift of the Holy Ghost."* So repentance and a water baptism in the name of Jesus will open a door for the spirit of truth to begin his operation in our lives.

The spirit of truth will also convict you of things in your life that are not pleasing to God. This is the beginning of transformation, and he will give you the strength and guidance to quit your old nature step by step if you listen and obey Him.

Being Filled with the Spirit

You need to ask God to fill you with the Holy Spirit after you are delivered from the spirit of sexual perversion because you cannot stay empty. Many find themselves back into sexual perversion after being delivered because they didn't welcome the spirit of God to fill that vacuum and to maintain their deliverance.

Matthew 12:43–45 says, *"When the unclean spirit is gone out of a man, he walks through dry places, seeking rest, and finds none. Then he says, I will return into my house from whence I came out; and when he is come, he finds it empty, swept, and garnished. Then goes he, and takes with himself seven other spirits more wicked than himself, and they enter in and dwell there: and the last state of that man is worse than the first. Even so shall it be also unto this wicked generation."*

When you don't get filled with the Holy Spirit after deliverance, it may cause you to fall back to a worse perversion state than you had at first.

Being filled with the Holy Spirit primarily means to be filled with the character and fruit of the Holy Spirit. Galatians 5:22–24 says, *"But the fruit of the Spirit is love, joy, peace, longsuffering, gentleness, goodness, faith, Meekness, temperance: against such there is no law. And they that are Christ's have crucified the flesh with the affections and lusts."* It requires a lot of diligence in reading the word of God, praying, fasting, and obeying God in everything to get the persistent fruit, power, and anointing of the Holy Spirit. It's the presence and infilling of the Holy Spirit that enables us to withstand temptations, thereby sustaining and perfecting our deliverance. Ecclesiastes 3:14 says, *"I know that, whatsoever God doeth, it shall be forever: nothing can be put to it, nor any thing taken from it: and God doeth it, that men should fear before Him."* God wants us to be perfected in his image (fruit of the spirit), which we lost when we opened a door for Satan's spirits to get into our lives.

Dreams and Visions

The spirit of truth communicates with us in various ways including dreams and visions. Whatever happens in the physical world first happens in the spiritual world. The spiritual world is permanent, and all spirits including our spirits, live forever. We are spirits, and we dwell in physical bodies. Whatever we do in the physical, we always first consider it consciously or subconsciously in the spirit. Our spirits are released into the spiritual world when we sleep, and whatever happens to our spirits during our sleep will manifest later in our physical bodies if it is not intercepted. God gives us a hint that what has happened, is happening, or is yet to happen before it is manifested in the physical world.

Isaiah 48:5 says, *"I have even from the beginning declared it to thee; before it came to pass I showed it thee: lest you should say, mine idol hath done them, and my graven image, and my molten image, hath commanded them."* We usually ignore our dreams, both good and bad, yet they will manifest in our lives at some point in the future.

The spiritual world has two kingdoms that are at war: God's kingdom against Satan's kingdom. Each of us belongs to one of the two and is controlled by the kingdom we submit to. The fact that these kingdoms are spiritual, we usually connect with them in dreams/visions which is a spiritual communication system. Acts 2:17 says, *"And it shall come to pass in the last days, saith God, I will pour out of my Spirit upon all flesh: and your sons and your daughters shall prophesy, and your young men shall see visions, and your old men shall dream dreams."*

One may have a dream about something hurting them in the chest and wake up with chest pain. However, this person will not get a proper diagnosis when he goes to the doctor. The pain that manifests in the physical was inflicted in the spiritual realm, and it is only God who can diagnose spiritual problems. It is advisable to seek a spiritual solution for a problem that manifests after a dream before seeking a physical solution. Many people don't care about dreams because of they are illiterate about them or because some people use them to mislead others, but Jeremiah 23:26–28 says, *"How long shall this be in the heart of the prophets that prophesy lies? yea, they are prophets of the deceit of their own heart; which think to cause my people to forget my name by their dreams which they tell every man to his neighbour, as their fathers have forgotten my name for Baal. The prophet that hath a dream, let him tell a dream; and he that hath my word, let him speak my word faithfully. What is the chaff to the wheat? saith the Lord."* Here we see dreams being compared to chaff and the word of God to wheat. Wheat comes embedded in chaff, we remove the wheat and trash the chaff, therefore it is important to ask God to help you get his word [message] out of the dreams we get.

There are basically three types of dreams:

   I.   Dreams from your mind – these happen when you see, think, or talk about something that strikes your mind. When you sleep, the part of the mind that doesn't sleep will draw your spirit into that experience in a dream. Isaiah 29:8 says, *"It shall even be as when an hungry man dreams, and, behold, he eats; but he awakes, and his soul is empty: or as when a thirsty man dreams, and, behold, he drinks; but he awakes, and, behold, he is faint, and his soul hath appetite."* You will need to clean your mind by reading the word of God and forsake watching, talking, or listening to evil things to avoid these kinds of dreams.

  II. Dreams from Satan – when you sleep and your spirit meets with demonic spirits. These evil spirits intend to harm your spirit in anyway, and their effect may manifest immediately or after a while in the physical. Evil spirits appear in our dreams in various ways, including dead people (relatives), fierce animals, scary faces, weird places (scenarios) and many others. Job had nightmares that manifested into him loosing all his belongings. Job 7:13–14 says, *"When I say, My bed shall comfort me, my couch shall ease my complaint; Then you scare me with dreams, and terrify me through visions."* We can avoid such dreams by cutting off all satanic ties and dedications.

III. Dreams from God – when your spirit meets with the spirit of God in your dreams. The Holy Spirit will reveal to you what God's plan is for your life or guide you in decision making to fulfill God's purpose for your life. Job 33:14–18 says, *"For God speaks once, yea twice, yet man perceives it not. In a dream, in a vision of the night, when deep sleep falls upon men, in slumbering upon the bed; Then he opens the ears of men, and seals their instruction, That he may withdraw man from his purpose, and hide pride from man. He keeps back his soul from the pit, and his life from perishing by the sword."*

Most dreams are usually in parables and are hard to decipher without spiritual revelation. Matthew 13:10–11 says, *"And the disciples came, and said unto Jesus, Why speak thou unto them in parables? He answered and said unto them, Because it is given unto you to know the mysteries of the kingdom of heaven, but to them it is not given."*

It is always for our benefit to ask the Lord to give us the spirit of revelation in dreams and visions so that we understand them like Daniel. Daniel 1:17 says, *"As for these four children, God gave them knowledge and skill in all learning and wisdom: and Daniel had understanding in all visions and dreams."*

A vision can be from God or Satan in the form of an audible voice or a trance. An understanding and confirmation of the vision can be achieved when you continue seeking God and praying deeper in the spirit.

Witness Protection Program

The spirit of truth provides special protection to those delivered from sexual perversion because they are a great asset to the kingdom of God. They are witnesses to God's supremacy, of being able to do all things, and they show his praise to the world.

Isaiah 43:9–12 says, *"Let all the nations be gathered together, and let the people be assembled: who among them can declare this, and show us former things? let them bring forth their witnesses, that they may be justified: or let them hear, and say, It is truth. You are my witnesses, says the LORD, and my servant whom I have chosen: that you may know and believe me, and understand that I am he: before me there was no God formed, neither shall there be after me."*

The spirit of truth declares that He alone can save and deliver a person; no other god can testify to this. Demons want you to believe that your transformation is impossible, but the God of truth has witnesses to prove that with him all things are possible.

The devil tries spiritually or physically to hinder witnesses from declaring the truth of what God has done for them, but the spirit of truth will provide guidance and protection for them till they fulfil God's purpose of deliverance. The devil plotted to kill Apostle Paul to stop him from witnessing in Rome as he had done in Jerusalem.

Acts 23:11 says, *"And the night following the Lord stood by Paul, and said, be of good cheer, Paul: for as thou hast testified of me in Jerusalem, so must thou bear witness also at Rome."*

The Lord talked to Paul in a dream, urging him to also witness of him in Rome. Your protection is assured when you go where God has asked you to go. The devil will use spiritual forces (sorcery and witchcraft) or people (agents promoting sexual perversions) to kill witnesses.

Acts 23:12–13, 16, 23–24 says, *"And when it was day, certain of the Jews banded together, and bound themselves under a curse, saying that they would neither eat nor drink till they had killed Paul. And they were more than forty which had made this conspiracy. Verse 16 says: And when Paul's sister's son heard of their lying in wait, he went and entered into the castle, and told Paul. And he called unto him two centurions, saying, Make ready two hundred soldiers to go to Cæsarea, and horsemen threescore and ten, and spearmen two hundred, at the third hour of the night; And provide them beasts, that they may set Paul on, and bring him safe unto Felix the governor."*

God will always warn you about the enemy's plots where you need to act quickly and accordingly. You need to stay prayerful, establish a stable communication system with God, and learn how to fight spiritual battles to prevail against their manifestation in the physical.

Psalm 27:5 says, *"For in the time of trouble he shall hide me in his pavilion: in the secret of his tabernacle shall he hide me; he shall set me up upon a rock."* It is wise to be sensitive to people's advice, however, you have to test and prove that their message or support really comes from God.

Psalm 141:9–10 says, *"Keep me from the snares which they have laid for me, and the gins of the workers of iniquity. Let the wicked fall into their own nets, whilst that I withal escape."* Wicked people may set snares like financial support, great job opportunities, travel opportunities, free housing, speaking engagements, scholarships, or any other help with an intention of bringing you back to sexual bondage or even kill you when you least expect it. So we need to watch, pray, and always inquire from the Lord about any opportunities presented to us, knowing that being a witness has a great reward from the Lord when you stand against all temptations.

Revelation 21:7 says, *"He that overcomes shall inherit all things; and I will be his God, and he shall be my son."* God will supply all your needs abundantly, including those you were denied because of forsaking sexual perversion if you maintain being a true witness before God in private and in public.

1 Corinthians 10:13 says, *"There hath no temptation taken you but such as is common to man: but God is faithful, who will not suffer you to be tempted above that ye are able; but will with the temptation also make a way to escape, that ye may be able to bear it."* It is good to ask the Lord for guidance about the people you meet and the opportunities that present itself to you. Take some time, at least take a night, before making critical decisions. This will give the Lord time to speak to you through his spirit of truth.

Numbers 22:7–8, 12–13 says, *"And the elders of Moab and the elders of Midian departed with the rewards of divination in their hand; and they came unto Balaam, and spoke unto him the words of Balak. And he said unto them, Lodge here this night, and I will bring you word again, as the LORD shall speak unto me: and the princes of Moab abode with Balaam. And God said unto Balaam, Thou shall not go with them; thou shall not curse the people: for they are blessed. And Balaam rose up in the morning, and said unto the princes of Balak, Get you into your land: for the LORD refuses to give me leave to go with you."*

One day, a pastor prophesied to me that the Lord wanted me to serve with him in his ministry. I asked him to give me some time so that I may also inquire of the Lord. I prayed about it, and that night I had a dream of that pastor hiding in a frog statue and trying to reach out to me. I didn't understand the dream, but when I went to my church, my pastor taught about false prophets and when we read scriptures, then I got the interpretation of my dream.

Revelation 16:13–14 says, *"And I saw three unclean spirits like frogs come out of the mouth of the dragon, and out of the mouth of the beast, and out of the mouth of the false prophet. For they are the spirits of devils, working miracles, which go forth unto the kings of the earth."* This proved to me that it was a false prophecy which manifested in form of a frog and it was intended to take me astray from the will of God. Therefore, always ask the Lord to speak to you concerning all matters of life.

Fresh Oil to Keep Burning

The power of the Holy Spirit (fresh oil) in your life is essential in sustaining your deliverance. This new anointing gives you endurance during challenging situations. Tougher challenges require more time to seek the Lord in prayer and fasting.

Our Lord Jesus was anointed for the ministry, yet He was challenged spiritually because of the cross that was set before Him.

His sorrow was an indication of the pressing need to seek his Father for fresh oil to strengthen Him go to the cross without fear.

Matthew 26:36–38 says, *"Then cometh Jesus with them unto a place called Gethsemane, and saith unto the disciples, Sit ye here, while I go and pray yonder. And he took with him Peter and the two sons of Zebedee, and began to be sorrowful and very heavy. Then says he unto them, My soul is exceeding sorrowful, even unto death: tarry ye here, and watch with me."*

A spiritual attack can be displayed through variety of different emotions, including anxiety, sorrow, worry, unforgiveness, bitterness, thoughts of fornication, stress, depression, confusion, suicidal thoughts, and many more. Any of these emotions are also an indication that you lack the spiritual empowerment (anointing) to withstand such situations or temptations. In such cases, we need to do what Jesus did, which was seeking the Lord for a fresh anointing to support you in your spirit so that you will stick to the will of God. If you fail to seek the Lord in a time of temptation, then you will give in to temptation and succumb to the will of the devil.

Luke 22:43–46 says, *"And there appeared an angel unto him from heaven, strengthening him. And being in an agony he prayed more earnestly: and his sweat was as it were great drops of blood falling down to the ground. And when he rose up from prayer, and was come to his disciples, he found them sleeping for sorrow, And said unto them, Why sleep ye? rise and pray, lest ye enter into temptation."* Jesus prayed earnestly and an angel came and strengthened Him. This new spiritual empowerment gave him peace and strength for the task which was ahead of him.

A lack of fresh anointing causes you to have dreams that are a reflection of your spiritual status. You may dream of having a sexual encounter, walking naked; climbing a mountain yet falling back; when not seeing your way, trying to do something but you are very weak; driving a vehicle but can't control it; or playing a game but can't score. All these are wake-up calls for seeking a fresh anointing.

Prayer

Father, in the name of Jesus, I am sorry for all the deception I have lived my life. I ask you to purge me with the blood of Jesus of all deceptive spirits.

Give me the fruit of your spirit to bring me back to the image of God so that I will be able have your godly character.

Lord, I ask for the spirit of truth to guide me and show me your will about my life in dreams and visions in Jesus's name.

Protect me, oh Lord, from all the wicked plans of the enemy and grant me the ability to testify to your greatness so as to bring back the lost to your kingdom.

Empower my spirit with your fresh oil, so I can stand against all temptations that I will be able to continue steadfastly in your will in Jesus' mighty name. Amen

23

If I Perish, I Perish

The spirit of sexual perversion has strong dominance over its victims and resents losing any to deliverance.

Genesis 19:5, 7, 9 says, *"And they called unto Lot, and said unto him, Where are the men which came in to you this night? Bring them out unto us, that we may know [have sexual relations with] them. And Lot said, I pray you, brethren, do not so wickedly. And they said, Stand back. And they said again, this one fellow came in to sojourn, and he wants to be a judge: now will we deal worse with you, than with them. And they pressed sore upon the man, even Lot, and came near to break the door."*

The spirit caused these men to be persistent and determined in their desire to have sexual relations with the angels who visited Lot in form of men. This spirit can cause some situations that discourage you from quitting, which may include death, rejection because you quit, unemployment, suicidal thoughts (thinking that you are better off dead), loss of favors and opportunities you had before your decision to quit, false accusations, imprisonment for no justifiable reason, and so much more.

The purpose of all this is to intimidate you to not to do the right thing, but if you are determined, the Lord will readily send you help. This happened to the nation of Israel: whenever they wanted to repent, unfavorable circumstances arose that hindered their decision.

Jeremiah 44:16–18 says, *"As for the word that thou hast spoken unto us in the name of the LORD; we will not hearken unto thee. But we will certainly do whatsoever thing goes forth out of our own mouth [or feelings], to burn incense unto the queen of heaven [spirit of sexual perversion], and to pour out drink offerings unto her, as we have done, we, and our fathers, our kings, and our princes, in the cities of Judah, and in the streets of Jerusalem: for then had we plenty of victuals, and were well, and saw no evil [resistance]. But since we left off [repented] to burn incense to the queen of heaven [spirit of lust], and to pour out drink offerings unto her, we have wanted all things, and have been consumed by the sword and by the famine."*

The people of Israel did not heed Jeremiah's message of repentance. They preferred to continue worshiping the queen of heaven, claiming that the calamity befell them whenever they turned back to God.

For this reason, Jesus encourages us in Revelation 2:9–10 by saying, *"I know your works [of repentance], and tribulation, and poverty, [but you are rich] and I know the blasphemy [false accusations] of them which say they are Jews [Christians or godly], and are not, but are the synagogue of Satan [representatives of Satan and his spirits]. Fear none of those things which you shall suffer: behold, the devil shall cast some of you into prison, that you may be tried; and ye shall have tribulation ten days [for a given period of time]: be you faithful unto death, and I will give you a crown of life.*

When I made the decision to repent and forsake sexual perversion, I was faced with enormous challenges, but thank God I was equipped with the knowledge of the word of God. I was rejected by previous friends because I no longer met their sexual needs, and I had cut ties with them to avoid slipping back to my old lifestyle. Fellow church members also forsook me, saying that I would contaminate them with the spirit of sexual perversion. The worst part of my tribulation was when my ex-wife packed her bags and left with my three-year-old son to a place unknown for several years. This marked the end of my ministry in Christian circles.

I had been a youth pastor yet struggling with homosexuality. However, after my deliverance, I was commanded by the Holy Spirit to share my story, which went viral on radio and TV, only to the disappointment of many who did not understand that the Lord wanted to use my story to minister to those suffering with sexual perversion. Because of my story, I had to lose my pastoral job, became homeless, slept on a church verandah, and survived on handouts.

Mark 8:38 says, *"Whosoever therefore shall be ashamed of Me and of My words in this adulterous and sinful generation; of him also shall the Son of man be ashamed, when he comes in the glory of his Father with the holy angels."*

Amid all of this, I never stopped sharing my story, kept praying for those struggling with homosexuality whenever I got opportunity in prisons and on public transports. I maintained a positive attitude toward the Lord because I knew he was with me.

Isaiah 43:1–2 says, *"But now thus says the LORD that created you, O Jacob, and he that formed thee, O Israel, Fear not: for I have redeemed thee, I have called thee by thy name; you are Mine. When you pass through the waters, I will be with you; and through the rivers, they shall not overflow you: when you walk through the fire, you shall not be burned; neither shall the flame kindle upon you."*

The only way to keep a positive attitude is by allowing God to speak to you through his word when you read the Bible and even through dreams. When the Israelites lost the ark of the covenant to the Philistines, it contained manna, Aaron's rod, and tablets which had the commandments. The ark and its contents represent you and me. It does not matter what situation(s) you may be going through as long as you keep the word of God (manna) in your heart and the power of God (Aaron's rod) we receive through seeking God (Fasting), plus the principles of the Lord (law tablets) in your walk, then you will surely be restored to glory as the ark was.

1 Samuel 5:2, 4, 7 says, *"When the Philistines took the ark of God, they brought it into the house of Dagon, and set it by Dagon. And when they arose early on the morrow morning, behold, Dagon was fallen upon his face to the ground before the ark of the LORD; and the head of Dagon and both the palms of his hands were cut off upon the threshold; only the stump of Dagon was left to him. And*

when the men of Ashdod saw that it was so, they said, the ark of the God of Israel shall not abide with us: for his hand is sore upon us, and upon Dagon our god."

After all the trials I went through, one day, the Lord spoke to me in a dream that I will be traveling to the United States for the ministry he has called me for. I believed that word and I blessed the Lord for it. A few months later as I was walking in downtown Kampala passing by an ATM machine, I saw that it had released some money for withdrawal, but there was no one at the machine. I stopped and checked; it was equivalent to $240 and a voice spoke to me that "this money is for your visa application." I was mesmerized because I had never heard of such a thing happening in a person's life. I obeyed the voice, took the money, and applied for a US visa, which was granted soon after. After getting my visa, the same voice asked me to visit a friend whom I had not seen for a while. I went to her store and told her what had happened at the ATM machine and also told her that I had been granted a US visa.

I also told her that I needed money for my ticket. The next day, she gave me the funds I needed for my air ticket. The Lord can do great things when we go through trials without denying His name.

Hebrews 10:35–36 says, *"Cast not away therefore your confidence, which hath great recompense of reward. For you have need of patience, that, after you have done the will of God, you might receive the promise."*

It's my prayer that you will not focus on what the devil will throw at you after quitting sexual perversion, but that you will despise the shame and set your eyes on the reward, which shall be granted to you by our Lord. Hebrews 12:2–4 says, *"Looking unto Jesus the author and finisher of our faith; who for the joy that was set before him endured the cross, despising the shame, and is set down at the right hand of the throne of God. For consider him that endured such contradiction of sinners against himself, lest ye be wearied and faint in your minds. Ye have not yet resisted unto blood, striving against sin."*

Prayer

Father, in the name of Jesus, I ask you to give me strength to repent and not look backward no matter the challenges.

Give me a positive attitude toward you, Lord, which will help me to focus on you only.

I surrender all my rights to you so that you will make a way for me to overcome every tribulation for your name's sake.

I dedicate my life to the blood of Jesus that only your will may be done in my life.

Help me through your Holy Spirit to keep your word, power, and principles that I may be able to share my story. In Jesus's mighty name. Amen.

24

Before You Celebrate

I understood the principle Jesus taught about evil spirits after I was delivered from homosexuality.

Matthew 12:43–45 says, *"When the unclean spirit is gone out of a man, he walks through dry places, seeking rest, and finds none. Then he says, I will return into my house from whence I came out; and when he is come, he finds it empty, swept, and garnished. Then goes he, and takes with himself seven other spirits more wicked than himself, and they enter in and dwell there: and the last state of that man is worse than the first. Even so shall it be also unto this wicked generation."*

The Lord gives us insight in this scripture on the process of deliverance. The spirit of sexual perversion leaves a person and comes back after some time to check on the person where it once lived in. If it finds that you do not have the word of God occupying your heart, mind, and body, it goes back and recruits more and stronger spirits to reoccupy your life. If that happens, then your life will actually become more perverted than before.

This brings our attention to what we need to do before, during, and after deliverance. True deliverance comes from prayer coupled with knowing the truth about the specific area where you need deliverance. Every believer needs to be totally delivered from whatever it was controlling their lives when they accepted Jesus Christ as their Lord.

Otherwise, you can remain in bondage, and it may result into the loss of the salvation you once attained.

We cannot be fellowshipping in the presence of the Lord while we live perverted lifestyles. Jesus described this to the Jews who believed in him.

John 8:31–35 says, *"Then said Jesus to those Jews which believed on Him [born-again Christians], if you continue in my word, then are you my disciples indeed; And ye shall know the truth, and the truth shall make you free [delivered]. They answered him, we be Abraham's seed, and were never in bondage to any man: how say you, you shall be made free [delivered]? Jesus answered them, verily, verily, I say unto you, whosoever commits sin is the servant of sin. And the servant [who keeps sinning] abides not in the house [presence of God] for ever: but the Son abides ever."*

Continuing in sin after believing in Jesus Christ means that you are still in bondage.

This is the truth the devil does not want the church to know. The Jews thought that they did not need deliverance as long as they believed in Jesus. However, Jesus assured them that continuing in sin reveals that one is still in bondage or under the control of another spirit which is not of God and, therefore, not a son of God.

Romans 8:14 says, *"For as many as are led [guided] by the Spirit of God, they are the sons of God."*

As a homosexual, it wasn't the spirit of the Lord leading me into sexual perversion. Many have experienced temporary relief after believing in the Lord Jesus Christ and have found themselves back in the same situation due to lack of the word of truth, which gives total freedom. This can make one think that it is impossible to be totally free from perverted lifestyles.

On one occasion, I received some temporary freedom from the spirit of sexual perversion after I read a book on how to overcome sin. I spent six (6) months without having any sexual affair with any guy, and I happily shared this with my ex-wife. Unfortunately, she was not convinced because, a couple of weeks later, I came back home only to find a note on our bed that she had decided to leave.

I became confused because I was not ready for this experience. I needed someone to talk to and became petrified that what was a family matter was going to become a public disgrace. I lost hope and needed someone to be there for me.

Unfortunately, the only people who were immediately available to talk to were my previous sexual partners since all church people were avoiding being named as one with me. This drew me back into homosexuality, and this time, it was worse than before because I had nothing to hide or protect.

I finally received total deliverance later, and now I know how to keep it because of the truth I have learned through the word of God.

When we continuously seek the Lord in prayer, fasting, and reading his word, we can be sure to avoid being drawn back into perverted lifestyles. Your life will be filled with the power of God, which will sustain you. Matthew 17:21 says, *"Howbeit this kind [of evil spirit] goes not out [or kept out after leaving] but by prayer and fasting."*

Your heart and mind must be filled with the word of God to keep you from falling back into sexual perversion. Psalm 119:11 says, *"Thy word have I hid in mine heart, that I might not sin against thee."*

The Lord will empower you to continue overcoming when you share your story of deliverance because your testimony gives other people hope to trust in the Lord for their own deliverance. Revelation 12:11 says, *"And they overcame him by the blood of the Lamb, and by the word of their testimony; and they loved not their lives unto the death."* Sharing your story is a great part of your deliverance.

Initially, as I prayed for deliverance, I had also purposed not to ever share my story for fear of retribution due to the general homophobic atmosphere in my country. But the Lord also made it clear to me that my deliverance depended on the condition that I would share my story as a service to him to bring many back into his presence.

Exodus 4:22–23 says, *"And you shall say unto Pharaoh, Thus says the LORD, Israel is my son, even my firstborn: And I say unto*

*thee, Let my son go, that he may serve me: and if you refuse to let
him go, behold, I will slay thy son, even thy firstborn."*

God delivered the children of Israel to serve him, and Jesus also
delivered the man controlled by a legion of demons for the same
reason, to serve him.

Mark 5:18–20 says, *"And when he was come into the ship, he that
had been possessed with the devil prayed him that he might be with
him. However, Jesus suffered him not, but said unto him, Go home
to thy friends, and tell them how great things the Lord hath done for
you, and has had compassion on you. And he departed, and began to
publish in Decapolis how great things Jesus had done for him: and
all men did marvel."*

I am sharing my story because I received instructions from the
Lord to make it public. However, the Lord also said that two things
are going to happen: He will touch people's lives through my story,
and they will be set free, and the enemy will also try to kill the story
with false accusations. I have witnessed this when a group of church
people from my own ministry left the church and began accusing me
of being sponsored by the gay community. I was not moved by this
because the Lord had fore warned me.

The Lord said that the enemy might try to destroy my life or set
traps to get me back into sexual perversion. The enemy tried to do
this with Lazarus, but he could not because Lazarus was usually in
Jesus's presence.

John 12:9–11 says, *"Much people of the Jews therefore knew that
he was there: and they came not for Jesus's sake only, but that they
might see Lazarus also, whom he had raised from the dead. But the
chief priests consulted that they might put Lazarus also to death;
because that by reason of him many of the Jews went away, and
believed on Jesus."*

The same evil spirits which wanted to kill Lazarus because of
his testimony are still operating through people today. They hate
seeing people go to Jesus because of your story; therefore, you must
be sober and vigilant everywhere you go. Dedicate your story, your

loved ones, and all your possessions under the blood of Jesus every time you share it and ask God to make your testimony permanent.

Ecclesiastes 3:14 says, *"I know that, whatsoever God does, it shall be forever: nothing can be put to it, nor any thing taken from it: and God does it, that men should fear before him."*

One day, I met a preacher who told me that it was so shameful for me to speak of such a terrible story. I never listened to him because I had decided to obey the Lord and not man. Mark 8:38 says, *"Whosoever therefore shall be ashamed of me and of my words in this adulterous and sinful generation; of him also shall the Son of man be ashamed when he cometh in the glory of his Father with the holy angels."*

On another occasion, as I shared my story, a church program manager came and pulled the microphone away from me and commanded me to sit down. I sat down without any resistance. Matthew 10:22–23 says, *"And ye shall be hated of all men for my name's sake: but he that endures to the end shall be saved. But when they persecute you in this city, flee ye into another: for verily I say unto you, Ye shall not have gone over the cities of Israel, till the Son of man be come."*

Another instance happened after I shared my story in a certain church and the pastor told me that the Lord wanted me to stay with his ministry, sleeping in the church for a whole year without sharing my story. But when I prayed, the Lord told me that it was a lie and a trick of the enemy to stop me from sharing my story.

Isaiah 59:15 says, *"Yes, truth fails; and he that departs [repents] from evil makes himself a prey: and the LORD saw it, and it displeased him that there was no judgment."*

Prayer

Father, in Jesus's name, I ask you to reveal to me the areas of my life where I need deliverance.

Give me the knowledge I need to receive my deliverance and guide me through your Holy Spirit to the right people and place where I will receive and maintain my deliverance.

Lord, help me to keep seeking you even after deliverance through prayer, fasting, and reading your word so that I will not be drawn back into perversion.

Lord, help me to share my story so that I bring back many souls to you for deliverance.

Lord, protect me from all plans of the enemy, which he has set to cause me to draw back toward sexual perversion.

Maintain my deliverance by filling me with your spirit and word so that my house will be fully occupied to hinder evil from retuning in Jesus's mighty name. Amen.

25

I Pledge Allegiance

The spirit of sexual perversion did not leave immediately after the man of God prayed with me, but because he taught me the truth of the word, I understood that I needed to continue seeking the Lord for my total deliverance. One day, the same minister read a scripture which forever changed my life.

Exodus 4:22–23 says, *"And you shall say unto Pharaoh, thus says the LORD, Israel is my son, even my firstborn: And I say unto you, Let my son go, that he may serve me: and if thou refuse to let him go, behold, I will slay thy son, even thy firstborn."*

God's command to the pharaoh (spirit of sexual perversion) was for the pharaoh to release his son so that the he may go and serve God. As I mentioned earlier, I had determined that I was not going to share my story because I did not want anyone to know about my struggle with homosexuality and did not want to be embarrassed or discriminated.

However, God's main purpose was to use my struggle and deliverance as a testimony to tell others that there is hope for deliverance from sexual perversion. John 12:42–43 says, *"Nevertheless among the chief rulers also many believed on Him; but because of the Pharisees they did not confess Him, lest they should be put out of the synagogue: For they loved the praise of men more than the praise of God."*

I had to choose between the praise of God and the praise of men. I was a youth minister and was known by many people in my country. My ex-wife was a gospel artist, and I had showcased in her music videos. With all this, I never wanted to lose my fame, yet I needed to make a godly decision with the help of scripture.

Job 22:27–30 says, *"Thou shall make thy prayer unto him, and he shall hear thee, and thou shall pay thy vows. Thou shall also decree a thing, and it shall be established unto thee: and the light shall shine upon thy ways. When men are cast down, then thou shall say, There is lifting up; and he shall save the humble person. He shall deliver the island of the innocent: and it is delivered by the pureness of thine hands."*

This scripture illustrates a process that had to begin with my prayer for deliverance and God hearing my prayer. I had to pay my vow to God and decree my deliverance, which was assured to be established. Then the light of the Lord would guide me how to keep my freedom.

Thereafter, I had to intercede for people oppressed by the spirit of sexual perversion, and the Lord would deliver them if I kept myself pure from defilement and temptations that may come in the process of ministering to others. However, I had failed the part of making a vow to God.

Psalm 116:16–18 says, *"O LORD, truly I am thy servant; I am thy servant, and the son of thine handmaid: thou hast loosed my bonds. I will offer to thee the sacrifice of thanksgiving, and will call upon the name of the LORD. I will pay my vows unto the LORD now in the presence of all his people."*

Using this knowledge, I made a vow to God that I would share my story all over the world if he delivered me from sexual perversion. I vowed to give a financial sacrifice of thanksgiving and to serve God by helping victims of sexual perversion to access their deliverance if the Lord would anoint me with unction to do it. One of the goals for this book is to fulfil my pledge to God, which was required for my total deliverance.

Many have lost their deliverance along the way because of not following through with what the Lord requires of them. Luke 17:15–19 says, *"And one of them, when he saw that he was healed, turned back, and with a loud voice glorified God, And fell down on his face at his feet, giving him thanks: and he was a Samaritan. And Jesus answering said, Were there not ten cleansed? but where are the nine? There are not found that returned to give glory to God, save this stranger. And he said unto him, Arise, go thy way: thy faith hath made thee whole."*

When Jesus touched the blind man, he initially saw men like trees walking, but when Jesus touched him again, he received total restoration of his sight. Therefore, sometimes deliverance may be an instant encounter or a gradual process, but it has to be from worse to better.

Mark 8:23–25 says, *"And he took the blind man by the hand, and led him out of the town; and when he had spit on his eyes, and put his hands upon him, he asked him if he saw ought. And he looked up, and said, I see men as trees, walking. After that he put his hands again upon his eyes, and made him look up: and he was restored, and saw every man clearly."*

Jesus led the blind man out of the town because He knew that the blindness could return to him if he stayed in that very place (atmosphere) that caused the blindness (bondage). Getting delivered is as important as maintaining deliverance after we get it.

Many of us want to be delivered, but we don't want to leave the peer groups, sexually perverted individuals, perverted places, perverted communities, perverted churches, perverted faiths, perverted traditions, perverted cultures, perverted programs, perverted careers, or any perverted atmosphere where we live. Yet these are the things that originally contributed to our bondage of sexual perversion.

Serving God and the Healing of Incurable Diseases

Victims of sexual perversion usually suffer from incurable

diseases, and this spirit exploits the agony to convince the victim that they are useless. The truth is that you are never useless when you are in God's hands. God is able to heal any disease (including HIV/AIDS, cancer, Coronavirus) you acquired as a consequence of the perversion. Those diseases may be a curse that came as a result of the sin of sexual perversion, but Jesus paid the price, and when you truly repent and walk in his ways, he will save you from sin and deliver you from the curse of incurable diseases.

Jeremiah 18:3–6 says, *"Then I went down to the potter's house, and, behold, he wrought a work on the wheels. And the vessel that he made of clay was marred in the hand of the potter: so he made it again another vessel, as seemed good to the potter to make it. Then the word of the LORD came to me, saying, O house of Israel, cannot I do with you as this potter? says the LORD. Behold, as the clay is in the potter's hand, so are ye in mine hand, O house of Israel."*

The Lord assures us that he can take care of every problem in our lives only when we are in His hands.

Exodus 15:26 says, *"And said, If thou wilt diligently hearken to the voice of the LORD thy God, and wilt do that which is right in his sight, and wilt give ear to his commandments, and keep all his statutes, I will put none of these diseases upon thee, which I have brought upon the Egyptians: for I am the LORD that heals thee."*

All diseases are curable because they have their origin in the spiritual world. That's why we need to seek the Lord about any sickness and not only depend on physicians.

2 Chronicles 16:12–13 says, *"And Asa in the thirty and ninth year of his reign was diseased in his feet, until his disease was exceeding great: yet in his disease he sought not to the LORD, but to the physicians. And Asa slept with his fathers, and died in the one and fortieth year of his reign."*

Most diseases will manifest in a person's life after having strange dreams. These diseases are indicators of the effects from the spiritual world. Common dreams are usually about: people who died from the same disease, falling in a pit, flying in the air, seeing yourself carrying a coffin, being shot at, being bitten by a snake, being buried, falling from heights, a dead person feeding you or giving you a ride, and many others.

Every disease connects you to death and dead people in your dreams and bring the spirit of death into your life. But Jesus will cut off death and heal the sickness.

Joel 3:21 says, *"For I will cleanse their blood that I have not cleansed: for the LORD dwells in Zion."* All blood diseases can be cleansed from your blood by the Lord.

Matthew 8:16 says, *"When the evening was come, they brought unto him many that were possessed with devils: and he cast out the spirits with his word, and healed all that were sick."*

One of the greatest hindrances to healing is unforgiveness and not witnessing for people about Jesus Christ. God has promised to heal us after forgiving us. However, God cannot forgive us unless we also forgive those who have hurt us or infected us with such incurable diseases.

Mark 11:25–26 says, *"And when you stand praying, forgive, if ye have ought against any: that your Father also which is in heaven may forgive you your trespasses. But if ye do not forgive, neither will your Father which is in heaven forgive your trespasses."*

It is necessary to spend some time in fasting and prayer when you find it difficult to forgive. Unforgiveness is also a demonic spirit that can be cast out with the blood of Jesus. After you have forgiven, then ask God to forgive you and to heal you of any disease.

Psalm 103:2–3 says, *"Bless the LORD, O my soul, and forget not all his benefits: Who forgives all your iniquities; who heals all thy diseases."*

Serving the Lord by bringing people to Him by means of interceding and witnessing for them about Jesus Christ is a great step to your healing because God heals us so that we may live and continue serving Him. Exodus 23:25–26 says, *"And ye shall serve the Lord your God, and he shall bless thy bread, and thy water; and I will take sickness away from the midst of thee. There shall nothing cast their young, nor be barren, in thy land: the number of thy days I will fulfill."*

Prayer

Father, in the name of Jesus, I ask you to give me the ability to pledge my life to your service and to quit everything that has contributed to my bondage to sexual perversion.

Lord, I make a vow that if you deliver me from sexual perversion and all its consequences, I will serve you all the days of my life by bringing people to you.

Lord, I also vow to witness to your kindness toward me before a great congregation and give you a sacrifice of thanksgiving in Jesus's name.

Lord, in the name of Jesus, I ask you for the grace to forgive everyone who has infected me with incurable diseases.

I choose to forgive everyone who has hurt me so that you cleanse me of the spirit of unforgiveness with the blood of Jesus.

Lord, I ask you to cleanse my blood and heal every sickness in my body so that I may be a witness to the nations to what you can do. In Jesus's mighty name. Amen.

26

One Thing I Do—I beat my body

The spirit of sexual perversion renders you powerless (without control) over your body; this is called the dedication of the body. This means that your body is dedicated to the spirit of sexual perversion's control, which now dictates your feelings and desires even after your spirit has been delivered to the Lord. This is true about many men of God as illustrated in the Bible.

Zechariah the priest and his wife, Elizabeth, were blameless and served the Lord in righteousness, yet the spirit of barrenness held their bodies in captivity, and they couldn't bear any children. The Lord intervened and dealt with this spirit such that their bodies submitted to God's will concerning their lives.

Luke 1:5–7 says, *"There was in the days of Herod, the king of Judaea, a certain priest named Zacharias, of the course of Abia: and his wife was of the daughters of Aaron, and her name was Elisabeth. And they were both righteous before God, walking in all the commandments and ordinances of the Lord blameless. And they had no child, because that Elisabeth was barren, and they both were now well stricken in years."* These servants of God were blameless before the Lord, yet their bodies were still in bondage.

God desires that we have total deliverance in all the three parts of our being: spirit, soul, and body. Lack of deliverance to one of the parts will cause defilement to all parts of your being and may bring back to bondage your parts which were once delivered.

1 Thessalonians 5:23 says, *"And the very God of peace sanctify you wholly; and I pray God your whole spirit and soul and body be preserved blameless unto the coming of our Lord Jesus Christ."*

Zachariah's faith wavered due to the blame in their bodies (old in age). His confession expressed a lack of faith in the word of God that he received from the angel. He served the Lord with fear, well aware of their shortcoming: having no child.

Luke 1:74–76 says, *"That he would grant unto us, that we being delivered out of the hand of our enemies might serve him without fear, In holiness and righteousness before him, all the days of our life."*

Even after my deliverance, sensual feelings would still stir up in me whenever I was sharing my story, which was an indication that there was still blame in my body. The Lord revealed it to me later after an ardent prayer that the spirit of sexual perversion still had authority over my body. I needed to repent and cancel the covenant of dedication to that spirit which it had in my body.

Such covenants can suppress the natural feelings for the opposite sex in people who have been delivered. In such cases, the outside world may also doubt your deliverance because you will have no feelings for all genders.

The truth is that the body needs to be addressed in the deliverance of its individual parts; like the eyes, mouth, private parts, brain, skin and breasts.

Jude 1:7–9 says, *"Even as Sodom and Gomorrah, and the cities about them in like manner, giving themselves over to fornication, and going after strange flesh, are set forth for an example, suffering the vengeance of eternal fire. Likewise also these filthy dreamers defile the flesh, despise dominion, and speak evil of dignities. Yet Michael the archangel, when contending with the devil he disputed about the body of Moses, durst not bring against him a railing accusation, but said, The Lord rebuke thee."*

Our bodies are defiled by our evil lifestyles. Satan claimed for Moses's body even after his death. Satan's accusation was that Moses' body was defiled, and it was in covenant with the gods of Egypt during his service to the pharaoh.

Acts 7:20–22 says, *"In which time Moses was born, and was exceeding fair, and nourished up in his father's house three months: And when he was cast out, Pharaoh's daughter took him up, and nourished him for her own son. And Moses was learned in all the wisdom of the Egyptians, and was mighty in words and in deeds."* Here we realize that Moses used his mouth and actions of his body to serve the Egyptian gods mightily.

I remember that I had to fight for the deliverance of my mouth because I had used it for oral sex during sexual perversion. After the deliverance of my spirit and soul, I could yet find interest in speaking perversely in conversations until I understood that my mouth was in covenant to be used by the spirit of sexual perversion.

God had to send in Michael the arch angel to deliver Moses's body from the devil's authority. Likewise, we need to ask God to send Michael to deliver our bodies (addressing individual parts) from the authority of this spirit of sexual perversion. But this can only happen when your spirit is born again and your name is written in the Lamb's book of life.

Daniel 12:1 says: *"And at that time shall Michael stand up, the great prince which stands for the children of thy people: and there shall be a time of trouble, such as never was since there was a nation even to that same time: and at that time thy people shall be delivered, every one that shall be found written in the book."*

It is reasonable service when you serve the Lord with your spirit, soul and body. At the same time, it is possible to serve the Lord with your spirit yet your body is serving the desires of the spirit of perversion. However, you will never make it to heaven with this kind of service because our actions will follow our spirits after this life to the judgment.

Matthew 7:21-23 says: *"Not everyone that says unto me, Lord, Lord, shall enter into the kingdom of heaven; but he that does the will of my Father which is in heaven. Many will say to me in that day, Lord, Lord, have we not prophesied in thy name? and in thy name have cast out devils? and in thy name done many wonderful works? And then will I profess unto them, I never knew you: depart from me, you that work iniquity."* This affirms the importance of your body's deliverance.

The Holy Spirit through Apostle Paul pleads with us to submit our bodies to God as reasonable service. Romans 12:1 says: *"I beseech you therefore, brethren, by the mercies of God, that ye present your bodies a living sacrifice, holy, acceptable unto God, which is your reasonable service."*

Sacrificing your body to God means denying yourself of things that would arouse your body to fight (go contrary to) your spirit, which denial is also known as killing the body.

When your spirit is stronger than your body it will control your actions. Conversely, a stronger body will draw you into submitting to the works of your body which are contrary to the spirit. Apostle Paul continues to tell us that when he serves the Lord in spirit, he subdues (denies) the body so that he may not be disqualified from attaining the heavenly reward.

1 Corinthians 9:26-27 says: *"I therefore so run, not as uncertainly; so fight I, not as one that beats the air: But I keep under my body, and bring it into subjection: lest that by any means, when I have preached to others, I myself should be a castaway."*

We subdue the body by denying it anything that stimulates actions of perversion. Things that stimulate the body are detailed in the chapter named "seeds will grow". Your body can cause you to do things which you know are evil when it is stronger than your spirit. Therefore in whatever you do, purpose to empower your spirit and weaken the body in order to win the battle.

Romans 7:15-18 says: *"For that which I do I allow not: for what I would, that do I not; but what I hate, that do I. If then I do that which I would not, I consent unto the law that it is good. Now then it is no more I that do it, but sin that dwells in me. For I know that in me (that is, in my flesh,) dwells no good thing: for to will is present with me; but how to perform that which is good I find not."*

Sin is innate in us and fights the righteousness of God in our spirit; the Holy Spirit in you will strengthen your spirit to fight back. The works of the body can only be subjugated by the Spirit of the Lord.

Romans 8:13–14 says, *"For if ye live after the flesh, ye shall die: but if ye through the Spirit do mortify the deeds of the body, ye shall live. For as many as are led by the Spirit of God, they are the sons of God."*

In Jesus's humanity he was also subjected to the works of the flesh. Jesus prayed and fasted to be filled with the power of the Holy Spirit to overcome the works of the flesh.

Luke 3:21–22 says, *"Now when all the people were baptized, it came to pass, that Jesus also being baptized, and praying, the heaven was opened, And the Holy Ghost descended in a bodily shape like a dove upon him, and a voice came from heaven, which said, Thou art my beloved Son; in thee I am well pleased."*

Luke 4:1-2 says: *"And Jesus being full of the Holy Ghost returned from Jordan, and was led by the Spirit into the wilderness, Being forty days tempted of the devil. And in those days He did eat nothing: and when they were ended, he afterward hungered."*

The devil tempted Jesus with material things to stimulate his body. Jesus did not yield to the devil's advances because he was filled with the power of the Holy Spirit and he overcame all the temptations. This is a true and great example of what we are supposed to do when we face the devil.

Luke 4:14 says: *"And Jesus returned in the power of the Spirit into Galilee: and there went out a fame of Him through all the region round about."*

Anyone who professes that he belongs to Christ has to follow his steps on how he dealt with temptation. Galatians 5:24 says: *"And they that are Christ's have crucified the flesh with the affections and lusts."*

The apostles tried to serve the Lord without following in His footsteps and the results were devastating. Matthew 17:19-21 says: *"Then came the disciples to Jesus apart, and said, Why could not we cast him out? And Jesus said unto them, Because of your unbelief:*

for verily I say unto you, If ye have faith as a grain of mustard seed, ye shall say unto this mountain, Remove hence to yonder place; and it shall remove; and nothing shall be impossible unto you. Howbeit this kind goes not out but by prayer and fasting."

Jesus explained that there are some demonic spirits which can be cast out by faith and prayer; and that there are others which are stronger and will require fasting and prayer for total deliverance.

For this reason we are commanded to make it a lifestyle to always seek the Lord and his power. Whenever your body urges you to act in ways contrary to the will of God, it is an indication that you need to fast. This could be for a period of time like 12hrs, 24hrs, or 72 hours and more as the Lord grants you the ability.

Psalm 105:4 says: *"Seek the LORD, and his strength: seek his face evermore."*

Calling upon the blood of Jesus to cleanse your conscience and reading the word of God (Bible) on a daily basis renews your mind and frees you from perverted spirits. God's word erases all the deposits of this spirit from the five corners of our mind which are: our wisdom, motives, interpretation, decision making and memory.

Hebrews 9:13-14 says: *"For if the blood of bulls and of goats, and the ashes of an heifer sprinkling the unclean, sanctifies to the purifying of the flesh: How much more shall the blood of Christ, who through the eternal Spirit offered himself without spot to God, purge your conscience from dead works to serve the living God?"*

Colossians 3:16 says, *"Let the word of Christ dwell in you richly in all wisdom; teaching and admonishing one another in psalms and hymns and spiritual songs, singing with grace in your hearts to the Lord."*

In order to break our body's dedication to the spirit of sexual perversion we ought to take these steps:

A. Repent on behalf of; our family (if it is a family spirit), our neighborhood (if it is a territorial spirit), those who bewitched us (if it was through sorcery), those who seduced or molested us (if it was due to forced sexual activity), using the blood of

Jesus to secure pardon for that sin. The blood of Jesus is able to cleanse our minds and then we replace whatever was in the mind with the word of God.

B. We must repent of the covenant in our body with that spirit through the given avenues, denounce its actions and sexual covenants and cancel them with the blood of Jesus. This will end the spirit's legal authority over your body.

C. Dedicate your body into the covenant of the blood of Jesus spiritually (by verbally drinking the blood of Jesus and eating his body) and physically (through Holy Communion).

D. Cast that spirit out of your body (you may touch the individual part of your body you are praying for, never allow anyone to touch your sensitive body parts in prayer) in the name of Jesus Christ. You can also ask the Lord to send the great Prince Michael to contend with this spirit for your body or body parts as he did for Moses.

E. After casting out the spirit of sexual perversion then ask the Holy Spirit to take its place in your body.

Romans 8:11 says, *"But if the Spirit of him that raised up Jesus from the dead dwell in you, he that raised up Christ from the dead shall also quicken your mortal bodies by his Spirit that dwells in you."*

Prayer

Father, in the name of Jesus, I repent on my own behalf, on the behalf of my family, on the behalf of my seducers, on the behalf of my molesters, on the behalf of my neighborhood, and on the behalf of those who bewitched me into dedicating my body to the spirit of sexual perversion.

We repent the covenants and sacrifices we made with our bodies, and we cancel them with the blood of Jesus Christ. We denounce all things we did with our body parts and dedicate our bodies to the covenant on the blood of Jesus.

Lord, deliver my body from the authority and prisons of the spirit of sexual perversion and bring my body parts from its custody in Jesus's name.

Lord, wash all my body parts with the blood of the lamb and break away all seals of satanic ownership from them.

In the name of Jesus, I cast out the spirit of sexual perversion from my eyes, from my mouth, from my hands, from my breasts, from my skin, from my private parts, from my legs, and from my entire body with the blood of Jesus.

Let Michael the archangel contend with the spirit of sexual perversion for my body and all its body parts that they may be delivered out of the spirit of sexual perversion's services and to the sacred service of the Lord Jesus Christ.

Father, I sanctify the Lord Jesus within my body and in my spirit, which I offer to Him to be His own. Restore all my God-given senses and natural feelings in Jesus's name.

Lord, fill my body with your Holy Spirit that I may serve you without fear, in righteousness and holiness all the days of my life. In Jesus's mighty name. Amen.

27

The Reward for the Walk

I have come to realize that, in life, there is a good or bad reward for every action. God gave us free will to choose what we want to do, but we do not have the choice of the consequences which come thereafter.

The reward for my sexually perverted lifestyle was the loss of my marriage, dignity, career, and friends. It was until five years of solitary life elapsed after my deliverance that I really understood the meaning of the scripture concerning sexual perversion.

Proverbs 6:32–33 says, *"But whoso commits adultery with a woman lacks understanding: he that does it destroys his own soul. A wound and dishonor shall he get; and his reproach shall not be wiped away."*

Sexual perversion destroys your own soul and causes heartbreak and dishonor. Even after my deliverance, many doubted whether I was really free and could not see the change in me because it was spiritual first. I could not make new male friends in church because they were forewarned of the outcome should they become my friends. This broke my heart, but I was comforted by God's presence, which I always felt whenever I turned to Him in prayer. He encouraged me that it was just for a short time.

James 1:12 says, *"Blessed is the man that endures temptation: for when he is tried, he shall receive the crown of life, which the Lord hath promised to them that love him."*

One heartbreaking instance was when I gave a ride to a friend's son to work. Someone saw me with this young man in the car and called his dad with a warning that his son was treading on dangerous grounds by sitting in my car. But since his dad was my friend and he already knew my story, he brought it to my attention to be aware of my image among the people. I thank the Lord that I was able to go through all this. But it has not been the same with many of our brothers and sisters who couldn't stand the testing moments. Many have let Satan deceive them into committing suicide. Suicide is not a solution. It's like avoiding the temporary pain and succumbing to eternal anguish.

Secondly, I lost my job as a church minister which led to bankruptcy with no provision for my necessities and I went hungry almost every day. This created a heart of compassion in me for people going through difficult moments in life irrespective of the cause.

Deuteronomy 8:3–4 says, *"And you shall remember all the way which the LORD thy God led thee these forty years in the wilderness, to humble thee, and to prove thee, to know what was in your heart, whether thou would keep his commandments, or no. And he humbled thee, and suffered thee to hunger, and fed thee with manna, which thou knew not, neither did thy fathers know; that he might make thee know that man doth not live by bread only, but by every word that proceeds out of the mouth of the LORD doth man live."*

Consequences of sexual perversion:

1. Loss of godly inheritance – God has already prepared a spiritual and physical inheritance/blessing for you when you walk in the path He designed for your life. This means that you will miss this benefit if you choose to walk in the path of the ungodly. A sexually perverted lifestyle is one of the ungodly paths that ends in self-destruction.

Hebrews 12:16–17 says, *"Lest there be any fornicator, or profane person, as Esau, who for one morsel of meat sold his birthright. For ye know how that afterward, when he would have inherited the blessing, he was rejected: for he found no place of repentance, though he sought it carefully with tears."*

Esau did not inherit his blessing because he didn't find time to repent and turn away from his lifestyle. All the things we get as benefits of living a life of sexual perversion are mere morsels (small pieces of food) in God's sight. The enemy sets these traps to lure you into a place of endless tears.

2. Punishment for rebellion – The consequence of rebellion after God has revealed his will for you is punishment. The word "stripes" in scripture signifies problems or adversities that the Lord will allow a person who refuses to abide by His truth and commandments to overtake.

Luke 12:47 says, *"And that servant, which knew his lord's will, and prepared not himself, neither did according to his will, shall be beaten with many stripes."*

Psalm 50:22 says, *"Now consider this, ye that forget God, lest I tear you in pieces, and there be none to deliver."*

These adversities can come in the form of sickness, poverty, failures, loss of great opportunities, loss of loved ones, natural calamities without a natural solution. In such moments, even the people with whom you share the same sexual lifestyle will turn away from you because no one can fight the hand of God.

Hosea 2:10 says, *"And now will I discover her lewdness in the sight of her lovers, and none shall deliver her out of mine hand."*

Ezekiel 7:19 says, *"They shall cast their silver in the streets, and their gold shall be removed: their silver and their gold shall not be able to deliver them in the day of the wrath of the LORD: they shall not satisfy their souls, neither fill their bowels: because it is the stumbling block of their iniquity."* In such moments also, your money will not be a solution if it has been the stumbling block hindering you from turning to the Lord.

3. Unanswered prayer – Our prayers become an abomination before the Lord when we refuse to hearken unto his will for our lives. A prayer of repentance and turning away from that which is not pleasing to God is the only acceptable prayer.

James 4:3–4 says, *"You ask, and receive not, because you ask amiss, that ye may consume it upon your lusts. Ye adulterers and adulteresses know you not that the friendship of the world is enmity with God? Whosoever therefore will be a friend of the world is the enemy of God."*

We shall not receive anything in prayer from God when our purpose is to enhance our evil desires or sexual perversions. Satan may give you provision for the purpose of reinforcing his evil plans in your life, but you should be aware that all he does for you is at the expense of your soul.

Proverbs 1:24–29 says, *"Because I have called, and ye refused; I have stretched out my hand, and no man regarded; But ye have set at naught all my counsel, and would none of my reproof: I also will laugh at your calamity; I will mock when your fear cometh; when your fear cometh as desolation, and your destruction cometh as a whirlwind; when distress and anguish cometh upon you. Then shall they call upon me, but I will not answer; they shall seek me early, but they shall not find me: For that they hated knowledge, and did not choose the fear of the LORD."*

4. Loss of identity – All creation has a God-given identity and so has man. The spirit of sexual perversion has manipulated people's identities by instilling vile affections that cause some to feel differently from their God-given identity. When we are sexually perverted, then we lose our God-given identity and enjoy for a season that which is against human nature. This can result in permanent change of gender through surgery,

but in the end, it will produce regret because feelings will change according to who is playing them. God has interest in what we do with every part of our body, that's why He has each of them recorded in His book.

Psalm 139:16 says, *"Your eyes did see my substance, yet being unperfected; and in thy book all my members were written, which in continuance were fashioned, when as yet there was none of them."*

God is also interested in how we dress because it carries part of our identity.

Deuteronomy 22:5 says, *"The woman shall not wear that which pertains unto a man, neither shall a man put on a woman's garment: for all that do so are an abomination unto the LORD thy God."*

Certain dress styles can be used by the spirit of sexual perversion or those who see you to lure you into sexual perversion. Many designers are dedicated to producing a fashion that work for Satan by identifying those who adopt them as sexual perverts or fashion that affects reproduction, causing people to become childless. You can catch the spirit of sexual perversion from such fashion or by sharing garments with someone who is possessed by this spirit.

5. Loss of eternal life – Sexual perversion will break our connection with God in this life and beyond. We will miss God's kingdom if we do not repent and turn away from this lifestyle.

1 Corinthians 6:9–10 says, *"Know you not that the unrighteous shall not inherit the kingdom of God? Be not deceived: neither fornicators, nor idolaters, nor adulterers, nor effeminate, nor abusers of themselves with mankind, Nor thieves, nor covetous, nor drunkards, nor revilers, nor extortioners, shall inherit the kingdom of God."*

2 Peter 2:4–6 says, *"For if God spared not the angels that sinned, but cast them down to hell, and delivered them into chains of darkness, to be reserved unto judgment; And spared not the old*

world, but saved Noah the eighth person, a preacher of righteousness, bringing in the flood upon the world of the ungodly; And turning the cities of Sodom and Gomorrah into ashes condemned them with an overthrow, making them an ensample unto those that after should live ungodly."

Rewards for Forsaking Sexual Perversion

There is a reward when you choose to repent and forsake sexual perversion.

1. Special grace – All of us are under the general grace of God who gives us physical life, rain, sunshine, and all the common things that God provides for us despite our lifestyles. But when you repent and keep the Lord's statutes, you will receive the special grace He reserves for only those that love Him and walk in His ways.

Matthew 5:45 says, *"That ye may be the children of your Father which is in heaven: for He makes his sun to rise on the evil and on the good, and sends rain on the just and on the unjust."*

1 Corinthians 2:9–10 says, *"But as it is written, eye hath not seen, nor ear heard, neither have entered into the heart of man, the things which God hath prepared for them that love him. But God hath revealed them unto us by his Spirit: for the Spirit searches all things, yea, the deep things of God."*

This scripture means that there are things that God does or reveals only to a few who choose to walk in His covenant. These include healing from incurable diseases, miraculous financial provision, great success in areas where other people are failing, great opportunities, protection for loved ones, and security from natural calamities.

Exodus 19:4–5 says, *"You have seen what I did unto the Egyptians, and how I bare you on eagles' wings, and brought you unto myself. Now therefore, if ye will obey my voice indeed, and keep my covenant, then you shall be a peculiar treasure unto me above all people: for all the earth is mine."*

2. Divine wisdom and skill – God will greatly reward you with wisdom and skill to do things beyond human intellect when you turn away from sexual perversion. This happened to me when I took the test for a class-A commercial driver's license with all endorsements here in the United States. I performed better than all the students in my class yet most of them were repeating the class. My tutor received a bonus for my excellent performance and told me that there is something special about me. God desires that you perform better in your area of operation. God also did this for some young men who purposed to repent and not defile themselves with the system in the kingdom of Babylon.

Daniel 1:8, 17–20 says, *"But Daniel purposed in his heart that he would not defile himself with the portion of the king's meat, nor with the wine which he drank: therefore he requested of the prince of the eunuchs that he might not defile himself. As for these four children, God gave them knowledge and skill in all learning and wisdom: and Daniel had understanding in all visions and dreams. Now at the end of the days that the king had said he should bring them in, then the prince of the eunuchs brought them in before Nebuchadnezzar. And the king communed with them; and among them all was found none like Daniel, Hananiah, Mishael, and Azariah: therefore stood they before the king. And in all matters of wisdom and understanding, that the king enquired of them, he found them ten times better than all the magicians and astrologers that were in all his realm."*

3. Divine exaltation – God will promote and exalt you in your area of expertise as he did for Joseph when he refused to sleep with his master's wife and disgrace himself.

Joseph suffered for a little while because of the false report against him, but God exalted him to the highest office in the land next to the pharaoh.

Genesis 41:38–41 says, *"And Pharaoh said unto his servants, Can we find such a one as this is, a man in whom the Spirit of God is? And Pharaoh said unto Joseph, Forasmuch as God hath showed thee all this, there is none so discreet and wise as thou art: Thou shall be over my house, and according unto thy word shall all my people be ruled: only in the throne will I be greater than thou. And Pharaoh said unto Joseph, See, I have set thee over all the land of Egypt."*

After repenting, you may go through challenging times socially, financially, or physically due to acquired illnesses, but these will not last. Romans 8:18 says, *"For I reckon that the sufferings of this present time are not worthy to be compared with the glory which shall be revealed in us."*

4. Double blessings – The Lord will grant you double blessings when you denounce Satan's ways. If your lifestyle was your profession and source of financial support, God surely understands and vows to compensate you.

Isaiah 40:1–3 says, *"Comfort ye, comfort ye my people, says your God. Speak you comfortably to Jerusalem, and cry unto her, that her warfare is accomplished, that her iniquity is pardoned: for she hath received of the LORD'S hand double for all her sins. The voice of him that cries in the wilderness, Prepare you the way of the LORD, make straight in the desert a highway for our God."*

There is a righteous way of doing godly things, which will bestow you with double blessings from the Lord. However, this particular way is not obvious to everyone because it requires you to lose some of your liberties, benefits, and many other things that may be regarded as normal.

Matthew 7:13–14 says, *"Enter you in at the strait gate: for wide is the gate, and broad is the way, that leads to destruction, and many there be which go in thereat: Because strait is the gate, and narrow is the way, which leads unto life, and few there be that find it."*

Some liberties or benefits may be provided by the law of the land, organizations, cultures, governments, etc. However, taking advantage of these liberties could become a stumbling block to the work of God in your life, including other people's lives.

1 Corinthians 8:9 says, *"But take heed lest by any means this liberty of yours become a stumbling block to them that are weak."* We should be aware and watchful against freedoms which are not acceptable by the Lord.

1 Corinthians 10:23 says, *"All things are lawful for me, but all things are not expedient: all things are lawful for me, but all things edify not."*

5. Deliverance from bad circumstances – Sexual perversion is an open door from which other demonic influences will enter your life. Sexual perversion is liken to a root of a tree, and bad circumstances are the leaves. Many people work hard to cut off the leaves, but as long as the root is not removed, the leaves will sprout again after a short while.

Job 14:7–9 says, *"For there is hope of a tree, if it be cut down, that it will sprout again, and that the tender branch thereof will not cease. Though the root thereof wax old in the earth, and the stock thereof die in the ground; yet through the scent of water it will bud, and bring forth boughs like a plant."*

A scent of water (seduction) to the root will cause the tree to thrive. It is essential to avoid things that bring back memories of sexual perversion to avoid returning to old habits. God wants us to keep our names in the book of life if we are to have access to total deliverance.

Daniel 12:1 says, *"And at that time shall Michael stand up, the great prince which stands for the children of thy people: and there shall be a time of trouble, such as never was since there was a nation even to that same time: and at that time thy people shall be delivered, every one that shall be found written in the book."*

Your name can be blotted out of the lamb's book of life and

disqualify you from total deliverance when you continue to sin (sexual perversion) after giving your life to the Lord. Revelation 3:19 says, *"He that overcomes, the same shall be clothed in white raiment; and I will not blot out his name out of the book of life, but I will confess his name before my Father, and before his angels."*

Prayer

Father, in the name of Jesus, I ask you to grant me the ability to make right decisions, knowing that whatever decision I make will have an outcome whether good or evil.

Lord, I repent the bad decisions I have made, which have resulted in pain, heartbreak, dishonor, poverty, and sicknesses.

Lord, forgive me and wash me by the blood of your son, Jesus Christ, from all the filthiness I have taken up with my sexual perversion.

Lord, I ask you to remove from me all consequences of sexual perversion as I purpose to walk in your ways hereafter.

Lord, I ask you to erase my name from the book of the dead and write my name in the lamb's book of life.

Lord, grant me special grace, divine exaltation, divine wisdom and skill, double blessings, and deliverance from bad circumstances in Jesus's name.

Lord, I declare that I am a special person to you beginning from my thoughts to my actions and ways in Jesus's mighty name. Amen.

28

My Perverse Loved One

My intention was not to break our marriage when I talked to my ex-wife about my homosexual quandary. I was drowning and needed a hand to help, but unfortunately, she had dealt with enough of my unfaithfulness and had made up her mind to quit the marriage one month after my confession.

Her response made me wonder whether it would have been better to keep silent forever and suffer my own guilt. This is one of the lies the spirit of sexual perversion applies to torment its victims. But the spirit of truth gives a different counsel.

Proverbs 28:13 says, *"He that covers his sins shall not prosper: but whoso confesses and forsakes them shall have mercy."* Keeping quiet will keep you from prospering against your sin, but if you confess it to the right person, God will grant you mercy to forsake it.

James 5:16 says, *"Confess your faults one to another, and pray one for another, that ye may be healed. The effectual fervent prayer of a righteous man availeth much."* So here we see the qualification of the person to whom we are to confess our faults (sexual perversion) to. They must be righteous and fervent in prayer to attract divine intervention on your behalf to overcome sexual perversion.

Many spouses are victims to such circumstances and are living in torment and guilt, hiding something they need help with. The sole purpose for opening up should be confessing to forsake and not confessing to be accepted. Many are coming out of the closet about their sexual perversion to feel free living in the perversion without any guilt. However, scripture recommends coming out to completely forsake the lifestyle.

The motive of your confession will determine your heavenly reward. Confessing to forsake produces godly sorrow that works salvation while confession to be accepted produces worldly sorrow that ends in death.

2 Corinthians 7:10–11 says, *"For godly sorrow works repentance to salvation not to be repented of: but the sorrow of the world works death. For behold this selfsame thing, that ye sorrowed after a godly sort, what carefulness it wrought in you, yea, what clearing of yourselves, yea, what indignation, yea, what fear, yea, what vehement desire, yea, what zeal, yea, what revenge! In all things ye have approved yourselves to be clear in this matter."*

In addition, godly sorrow will cause you to be careful not to fall back into perversion and to avoid places or environments that stimulate lustful thoughts. In due time, you will have an indignation against sexual perversion but not at the victims.

The word of God reminds us that our struggle is not against each other but against the spiritual forces that influence the people.

Ephesians 6:12 says, *"For we wrestle not against flesh and blood, but against principalities, against powers, against the rulers of the darkness of this world, against spiritual wickedness in high places."*

Seeking Counsel

It is very important that you ask the Lord to guide you toward a trustworthy person for counseling, whether a spouse or friend. This will be evidenced by the fruit they bear in public and private. Please also note that not every spiritual minister has the necessary help you need. In fact, many ministers and counselors are also in need of help themselves.

I lived with my sexual perversion for quite a while because I never trusted the ministers around me until the Lord spoke to me in a dream about the minister who would counsel me. I have heard of cases where a person seeking for help is sexually abused instead; therefore, be cautious so as not to give yourself in more suffering.

It is very important to give detailed information as to the origin of the perversion in your life for your counselor to understand and give you counsel accordingly.

The purpose of this book is to be that true person who can help you with the mercies of the Holy Spirit. People who are ignorant, afraid, excited, judgmental, or condoning about the topic are not helpful counselors.

Giving Counsel

When someone approaches you, seeking for help about their sexual perversion, you need to have enough knowledge about that topic and also bear the fruit of the spirit called compassion. Having these two will give you the ability to help that individual. Isaiah 53:11 says, *"He shall see of the travail of his soul, and shall be satisfied: by his knowledge shall my righteous servant justify many; for he shall bear their iniquities."*

This person may have already been condemned, tormented, and on the verge of taking their life because that is all the spirit of sexual perversion offers.

Isaiah 57:20–21 says, *"But the wicked are like the troubled sea, when it cannot rest, whose waters cast up mire and dirt. There is no peace, says my God, to the wicked."*

You need to understand that this individual cannot help himself/ herself. You have to be compassionate because the Lord has entrusted you with his/her life.

Most people involved in sexual perversion usually put on an outward appearance of being happy and independent. But do not believe what you see. It's just a mask. They may also reject your help because of personal insecurities and experiences. However, you need to continue doing good to them until your good deeds break the barriers built around them by the spirit of sexual perversion.

1 Peter 3:16–17 says, *"Having a good conscience; that, whereas they speak evil of you, as of evildoers, they may be ashamed that falsely accuse your good conversation in Christ. For it is better, if the will of God be so, that you suffer for well doing, than for evil doing."*

We should also ask God for the spirit of endurance, which means having peace in heart and joy on the face when going through hard circumstances. This is a spiritual battle, and your spirit has to overcome the spirit of sexual perversion. If you have anger, unforgiveness, or any negative attitude toward the person seeking help, then you are not in position to help them. This is because anger is an evil spirit and sexual perversion is an evil spirit. The Satan of anger in you cannot overcome the Satan of sexual perversion in the other person.

Matthew 12:24, 26, 28 says, *"But when the Pharisees heard it, they said, This fellow doth not cast out devils, but by Beelzebub the prince of the devils. And if Satan cast out Satan, he is divided against himself; how shall then his kingdom stand? But if I cast out devils by the Spirit of God, then the kingdom of God is come unto you."*

The spirit of compassion and endurance will give you access to the power of God so you can cast out the spirit of sexual perversion.

2 Chronicles 16:9 says, *"For the eyes of the LORD run to and fro throughout the whole earth, to show himself strong in the behalf of them whose heart is perfect toward him."* God always wants to show his strength on the behalf of those with a perfect heart. This is the heart of Jesus's ministry. He has compassion for the victims of evil spirits.

Matthew 9:36–37 says, *"But when He saw the multitudes, He was moved with compassion on them, because they fainted, and were scattered abroad, as sheep having no shepherd. Then says He unto his disciples, The harvest truly is plenteous, but the laborers are few."*

This scripture illustrates how Jesus feels about the victims of sexual perversion. They are fainting, and they have no one to guide them out of their bondage. God is looking for compassionate laborers so that he may give them power and authority to prevail against the spirits of sexual perversion in the victims' lives.

When the children of Israel wanted to overcome the spirit of sexual perversion inside their loved ones (the children of Benjamin), they first tried fighting with anger inside them, and they lost the battle twice even if God was on their side and had given the green light to go and attack. It was until they acquired the spirit of compassion through fasting and repentance on the behalf of their loved ones that God gave them power and wisdom to overcome the spirit of sexual perversion (Read Judges chapters 19, 20, and 21).

Process to Administer Deliverance

1. Dedicate yourself to God through the blood of Jesus to cleanse yourself from all things that are not of the kingdom of God.

Hebrews 9:13–14 says, *"For if the blood of bulls and of goats, and the ashes of an heifer sprinkling the unclean, sanctifies to the purifying of the flesh: How much more shall the blood of Christ, who through the eternal Spirit offered himself without spot to God, purge your conscience from dead works to serve the living God?"*

2. Ask God for the spirit of grace and supplication. This will cause you to have compassion for the person you are interceding for. You should not discuss or speak evil about the person you are interceding for.

Zechariah 12:10 says, *"And I will pour upon the house of David, and upon the inhabitants of Jerusalem, the spirit of grace and of supplications: and they shall look upon me whom they have pierced, and they shall mourn for him, as one mourns for his only son, and shall be in bitterness for him, as one that is in bitterness for his firstborn."*

3. Forgive that person and forget what they have done. This person is now depending on your relationship with God to be reconciled with Him. Your unforgiveness as their intercessor means that God cannot also forgive them. It is important that you take time, fasting and praying, for God to grant you the grace to forgive if it becomes a challenge.

John 20:22–23 says, *"And when he had said this, he breathed on them, and says unto them, Receive ye the Holy Ghost: Whose so ever sins you remit, they are remitted unto them; and whose so ever sins you retain, they are retained."*

4. Repent on behalf of the person by confessing their perversion before God, saying, "Lord, we have sinned against you." This means that you are sanctifying yourself on behalf of the person you are interceding for. This will secure pardon for their sin before God.

John 17:19 says, *"And for their sakes I sanctify myself, that they also might be sanctified through the truth."*

5. Dedicate the person to the blood of Jesus. This means you have given the person over to Jesus Christ's authority. Jesus can now communicate with this person like he did with the heathen king who didn't know God.

Ezra 1:1–2 says, *"Now in the first year of Cyrus king of Persia, that the word of the LORD by the mouth of Jeremiah might be fulfilled, the LORD stirred up the spirit of Cyrus king of Persia, that he made a proclamation throughout all his kingdom, and put it also in writing, saying, thus says Cyrus king of Persia, The LORD God of heaven hath given me all the kingdoms of the earth; and he hath charged me to build him an house at Jerusalem, which is in Judah."*

6. Ask the Lord by the blood of Jesus to purchase them from the powers of deception and of sexual perversion. Ask the blood of Jesus to cleanse them from all filthiness. Repent and cancel all demonic covenants in their life, and dedicate them into the covenant with God through the blood of Jesus. Weaken the spirits of deception and sexual perversion by dragging them into the sea of the blood of Jesus. Undress the individual of the garment of deception and sexual perversion with the blood of Jesus. Ask God to bring the individual out of the prison of the spirit of sexual perversion through the blood of his covenant. The blood of Jesus is able to do whatever you want it to do. Apply it extensively because it is a living thing.

Zechariah 9:11 says, *"As for thee also, by the blood of thy covenant I have sent forth thy prisoners out of the pit wherein is no water."*

7. Call upon the Lord to rain brimstone and fire onto the spirit of deception and sexual perversion in the individual's life as He did in Sodom. Lastly, ask the Holy Spirit to dress the individual with the spirit of conviction and of truth. People change through conviction, not condemnation.

John 16:8, 13 says, *"And when He is come, He will reprove the world of sin, and of righteousness, and of judgment. Howbeit when he, the Spirit of truth, is come, He will guide you into all truth: for He shall not speak of himself; but whatsoever He shall hear, that shall He speak: and He will show you things to come."*

Due diligence and consistency are necessary when dealing with such spirits of perversion, and it will surely bring victory. 2 Samuel 3:1 says, *"Now there was long war between the house of Saul and the house of David: but David waxed stronger and stronger, and the house of Saul waxed weaker and weaker."* This proves that you need to continue to go through the deliverance process diligently until you acquire the desired goal.

The Canaanite woman pleaded diligently with Jesus for her

daughter, who was tormented by evil spirits (supposedly sexual perversion because the term "dogs" is usually used to express persons in that category) until Jesus delivered her daughter.

Matthew 15:26–28 says, *"But he answered and said, It is not meet to take the children's bread, and to cast it to dogs. And she said, Truth, Lord: yet the dogs eat of the crumbs which fall from their masters' table. Then Jesus answered and said unto her, O woman, great is thy faith: be it unto thee even as thou wilt. And her daughter was made whole from that very hour."*

Most times during our quest for the deliverance of our loved ones, there will be a backfire (spiritual or physical attacks) from these spirits, trying to punish you for helping their victim to go free, but you have to cover yourself, the victim, your people, and everything that belongs to you with the blood of Jesus all the time to hinder such instances.

For Spouses

Divorcing your spouse because of sexual perversion will not change them but, instead, will make you miss a great reward from the Lord, just like Lot's wife, who lost her destiny when she turned and looked back, not continuing with her husband unto a place of total deliverance. Genesis 19:26 says, *"But his wife looked back from behind him, and she became a pillar of salt."*

Lot's wife turned against the plan and the word of God that was spoken by the angels. She compromised the destiny of her daughters too because her absence in their lives opened the door to incest. Her daughters conspired to become sexually involved with their own father. Genesis 19:31–32 says, *"And the firstborn said unto the younger, Our father is old, and there is not a man in the earth to come in unto us after the manner of all the earth: Come, let us make our father drink wine, and we will lie with him, that we may preserve seed of our father."*

So many kids who have grown up with single parents have been compromised by the spirit of sexual perversion because they lack model parents to talk and look up to. Genesis 2:15–16 says, *"And did not he make one? Yet had he the residue of the spirit. And wherefore one? That he might seek a godly seed. Therefore take heed to your spirit, and let none deal treacherously against the wife [husband] of his youth. For the Lord, the God of Israel, saith that he hates putting away [divorce]: for one covers violence with his garment, saith the Lord of hosts: therefore take heed to your spirit, that ye deal not treacherously."*

Many couples have separated because of sexual perversion, being unaware that the enemy's plan was to destroy the destiny of their children. How do you know that you are in that marriage for such a time as this? For God to use you to bring deliverance to your spouse and children. You are God's beloved when you help someone turn back to God. The Lord will reward your work.

Isaiah 53:12 says, *"Therefore will I divide him a portion with the great, and he shall divide the spoil with the strong; because he hath poured out his soul unto death: and he was numbered with the transgressors; and he bare the sin of many, and made intercession for the transgressors."*

Prayer

Father, in the name of Jesus Christ, I dedicate myself in the blood of Jesus to cleanse me from all things that are not of the kingdom of God and ask you to give me the knowledge and compassion I need that I may be in position to minister deliverance to those you've put in my way and are tormented by sexual perversion.

Lord, remove from me all un-forgiveness, anger, bitterness, and judgmental spirits with the blood of your son, Jesus Christ.

Give me wisdom and a mouth that the spirit of sexual perversion can never gainsay nor resist in Jesus's name.

Empower my spirit with authority and the diligence of your Holy

Spirit so that I may never give up or get offended until I see your deliverance in your people.

I cover my life, my loved ones, and whatever concerns us with the blood of Jesus for our protection. In Jesus's mighty name. Amen.

29

Do I Qualify to Be Married?

Six years after my deliverance from homosexuality, the Lord told me that I should think about remarrying. I was shocked because I thought I had ruined my life forever when my ex-wife divorced me. I did not think that I had another chance of having an acceptable and genuine marriage in God's sight. I was not looking for something acceptable as for the government system, for I now knew that not everything legal by earthly standards is necessarily acceptable to God.

Malachi 2:13–16 says, *"And this have you done again, covering the altar of the LORD with tears, with weeping, and with crying out, insomuch that he regards not the offering any more, or receives it with good will at your hand. Yet you say, why? Because the LORD has been witness between you and the wife/husband of your youth, against whom you have dealt treacherously [unfaithfully]: yet is she your companion, and the wife of your covenant. And did not God make one? Yet had he the residue of the spirit. And why one? That he might seek a godly seed. Therefore take heed to your spirit, and let none deal treacherously [unfaithfully] against the wife of his youth. For the LORD, the God of Israel, says that he hates putting away [divorce]: for one covers violence with his garment, says the LORD of hosts: therefore take heed to your spirit, that you deal not treacherously."*

God gives us specific principles about marriage. He made one partner for every one so that, together, they might produce and raise godly offspring who would follow in their parents' footsteps.

God rejects offerings, ministry, and prayers offered by an unfaithful spouse, and finally, God hates divorce. I had been compelled by this scripture to sincerely ask my ex-wife for forgiveness and give me an opportunity for reconciliation, which she rejected.

I had approached my deliverance minister for counseling to help us get back together but it didn't work. He had asked me to spend more time in prayer for her that she would seriously consider saving our marriage. I waited for a period of four years, but her opinion of divorce did not change, and finally, she got it.

Later, I got advice from various sources which suggested celibacy for me until I read scripture, 1 Timothy 4:1–3, which says, *"Now the Spirit speaks expressly, that in the latter times some shall depart from the faith, giving heed to seducing spirits, and doctrines of devils; Speaking lies in hypocrisy; having their conscience seared with a hot iron; forbidding to marry, and commanding to abstain from meats, which God hath created to be received with thanksgiving of them which believe and know the truth."*

Celibacy is biblically acceptable for anyone who can abide by its restrictions and has never been involved in sexual perversion. Having been involved in a homosexual lifestyle was proof that I could not contain myself, and celibacy was not my gift from God. Matthew 19:10–12 says, *"His disciples say unto him, If the case of the man be so with his wife, it is not good to marry. But he said unto them, All men cannot receive this saying, save they to whom it is given. For there are some eunuchs, which were so born from their mother's womb: and there are some eunuchs, which were made eunuchs of men: and there be eunuchs, which have made themselves eunuchs for the kingdom of heaven's sake. He that is able to receive it, let him receive it."*

According to scripture, those who have been delivered from sexual perversion are entitled to holy matrimony. Judges 21:12–14, 23 says, *"And they found among the inhabitants of Jabeshgilead four hundred young virgins, that had known no man by lying with any male: and they brought them unto the camp to Shiloh, which is in the land of Canaan. And the whole congregation sent some to speak to the children of Benjamin (who had survived from the sodomy attack) that were in the rock Rimmon, and to call peaceably unto them. And Benjamin came again at that time; and they gave them wives which they had saved alive of the women of Jabeshgilead: and yet so they sufficed them not. And the children of Benjamin did so, and took them wives, according to their number, of them that danced, whom they caught: and they went and returned unto their inheritance, and repaired the cities, and dwelt in them."*

The children of Benjamin who were delivered from homosexuality were in celibacy for four months. After which, their brethren found them wives so that they are not tempted to return to their old lifestyle of committing sexual perversion because of sexual starvation.

1 Corinthians 7:2, 8–9 says, *"Nevertheless, to avoid fornication, let every man have his own wife, and let every woman have her own husband. I say therefore to the unmarried and widows, It is good for them if they abide even as I. But if they cannot contain, let them marry: for it is better to marry than to burn [return to sexual perversion]."*

The women given to those who were delivered were virgins, which signifies purity, meaning that it is advisable for a man who has been delivered from being gay to get a wife who has never been a lesbian, and for a woman who has been delivered from being a lesbian to get a man who has never been gay. This will not give the enemy a chance of separating you because, at least, one of you will cling to the other in times of temptation.

When the spirit of sexual perversion comes to check on you, it will have an advantage if both of you have been delivered from same-sex perversion. It would be easier for it to make the man lose feelings for the woman and, at the same time, make the woman lose feelings for the man as it was before their deliverance. In conclusion, a man delivered from sodomy should not marry a woman delivered from lesbianism.

There was a great battle when I got a wife to marry after my deliverance because the spirit of sexual perversion wanted to stay in control of my body through temptations of other forms of perversion (pornography and masturbation), which would be hard for it if I go into holy matrimony. Therefore, you should be aware when you see resistance to your marriage in the form of doubts about your deliverance, relatives of your new spouse not blessing the marriage, rumors discouraging your new spouse, the clergy refusing to join you in church, people refusing to support your wedding financially, being impotent after the wedding, closing of female marital organs to hinder intercourse, losing feelings for each other after the wedding, and many more. All these can be overcome by consistency in prayer as illustrated in the chapter, **"One Thing I Do, I Beat My Body."**

Hebrews 13:4 says, *"Marriage is honorable in all, and the bed undefiled: but whoremongers and adulterers God will judge."* Marriage between a man and a woman is honorable before God, and He blesses their bed. But God will judge those of us who continue to have sexual affairs with anyone not of the opposite sex and not the human marriage partner.

God is an integral part of marriage with the purpose of the couple serving him and producing Christ's nature so that people will see Christ through our marriages.

It is possible for you to be joined in marriage by the clergy in church, yet God has not joined you spiritually. Therefore, we need to ask God to reveal to us whom He has joined us with spiritually before we seek to be joined physically.

Matthew 19:6 says, *"Wherefore they are no more twain, but one flesh. What therefore God hath joined together, let not man put asunder."*

God may join you in marriage spiritually with someone whom you may not have love for or any mutual interests in at the beginning. The lack of love may be caused by our fleshly desires (financial status, educational background, family nonmarital bondages, physical appearances, cultural beliefs, race, or nationality). Yet if we choose to accept God's choice for us and pray for them, then He will eventually bless us according to His divine destiny for our marriage.

Matthew 1:19–20 says, *"Then Joseph her husband, being a just man, and not willing to make her a public example, was minded to put her away privately. But while he thought on these things, behold, the angel of the Lord appeared unto him in a dream, saying, Joseph, thou son of David, fear not to take unto thee Mary thy wife: for that which is conceived in her is of the Holy Ghost."*

God can show you your destined marriage partner by; a dream like he did with Joseph, speaking to you about them through another person or a conviction of the Holy Spirit. Each of these needs to a have a confirmation from another avenue to avoid making mistakes. Remember also that we can only get married to someone of the same faith as us in Christ because scripture warns about light not being able to be joined with darkness. 2 Corinthians 6:14–15 says, *"Be ye not unequally yoked together with unbelievers: for what fellowship hath righteousness with unrighteousness? and what communion hath light with darkness? And what concord hath Christ with Belial? or what part hath he that believeth with an infidel?"*

Childbirth

The spirit of sexual perversion schemes to hinder God's purpose for the unborn babies of people who have been delivered from sexual perversion by encouraging planned parenthood in their marriages. But remember, there are no coincidences for God regarding child conception. He knows our spirits before we are born and the conditions in which we would be born.

Psalm 139:13–16 says, *"For thou hast possessed my reins: thou hast covered me in my mother's womb. I will praise you; for I am fearfully and wonderfully made: marvelous are thy works; and that my soul knows right well. My substance [body structure] was not hid from you, when I was made in secret, and curiously wrought in the lowest parts of the earth. Your eyes did see my substance, yet being unperfected; and in thy book all my members were written, which in continuance were fashioned, when as yet there was none of them."*

God sees our body structure and documents every part of the body as it is formed in a mother's womb. Performing an abortion, changing our gender, or being an accessory in any form to the mentioned means that we are shedding innocent blood with our very hands. This will invite a blood curse into our lives and resulting in being rejected for no justifiable reason, lack of establishment in our endeavors, failure to get an increase in our investments, and above all, having unanswered prayers unless we genuinely repent.

Isaiah 1:15 says, *"And when ye spread forth your hands, I will hide mine eyes from you: yea, when ye make many prayers, I will not hear: your hands are full of blood."*

I heard a true story from a sister who got a vision of heaven. She saw children crying to God for judgment on their divinely ordained parents who refused to give birth to them through planned parenthood and by refusing to get married.

Prayer

Father, in the name of Jesus, I repent all mistakes I have made in marriage. I am sorry for joining myself with people or creatures you did not join me to in marriage.

I am sorry for changing the nature you designed for marriage. Forgive me for refusing your choice of marriage partner and give me a heart to accept what you ordained for me.

Lord, I repent any innocent blood that my hands has shed through abortion or genital mutilation with the intent of satisfying my fleshly desires. Forgive me, Lord, and wash away my sin with the blood of Jesus.

Lord, I ask you to purge me with the blood of Jesus and to lead me into your will concerning marriage so that I will do only that which is acceptable before you, being guided by your Holy Spirit. In Jesus's name. Amen.

30

My Christian Obligation

As a Christian or a person who loves the Lord, you are obligated to support what the Lord is doing by fighting the spirit of sexual perversion. The Lord requires us to get out of our sexual perversion with all our substance; therefore, we cannot support sexual perversion in any way.

Romans 1:32 says, *"Who knowing the judgment of God, that they which commit such things are worthy of death, not only do the same, but have pleasure in them that do them."*

God may judge us by our motives and what we have pleasure in or support. Many people are not involved in sexual perversion but they support it by advocating it; giving their donations; recruiting people into it; investing or working in companies which promote it, buying items used for sexual perversions; subscribing to channels promoting it; following social media accounts of agents of sexual perversion; using our God-given resources (houses, vehicles, equipment, votes, positions of authority) to enhance sexual perversion; and watching, liking, and sharing publications of sexual perversion etc.

When we do the above things, we get the same reward as those who practice sexual perversion. 2 Chronicles 19:2 says, *"And Jehu the son of Hanani the seer went out to meet him, and said to King Jehoshaphat, Shouldest thou help the ungodly, and love them that hate the Lord? therefore is wrath upon thee from before the Lord."*

God sent wrath to King Jehoshaphat [a child of God] because of supporting the works of Satan which were being done by King Ahab and his wife Jezebel [spirit of sexual perversion].

When the angels came to Sodom to deliver Lot from the spirit of sexual perversion, they instructed him not to leave anything that belonged to him under the control of that spirit. Genesis 19:12–13 says, *"And the men said unto Lot, Hast thou here any besides? son in law, and thy sons, and thy daughters, and whatsoever thou hast in the city, bring them out of this place: For we will destroy this place, because the cry of them is waxen great before the face of the LORD; and the LORD hath sent us to destroy it."*

Many people have lost their investments or resources because they supported things which God hates. Deuteronomy 7:26 says, *"Neither shall you bring an abomination into your house, lest you be a cursed thing like it: but you shall utterly detest it, and you shall utterly abhor it; for it is a cursed thing."* Your house represents your heart or your belongings. All these must not have anything in them which the Lord hates because whatever He hates is cursed. And whatever is cursed will be destroyed.

The battle against sexual perversion is one of the battles in Christianity where everyone is required to participate. If you choose to do nothing about it, you may get the same judgment as those that committed it.

Isaiah 65:12 says, *"Therefore will I number you to the sword, and ye shall all bow down to the slaughter: because when I called, ye did not answer; when I spake, ye did not hear; but did evil before mine eyes, and did choose that wherein I delighted not."*

The children of Israel were fighting against the spirit of homosexuality in the tribe of Benjamin, and those that didn't participate died just like those who practiced it.

Judges 21:8–10 says, *"And they said, What one is there of the tribes of Israel that came not up to Mizpeh to the LORD? And, behold, there came none to the camp from Jabeshgilead to the assembly. For the people were numbered, and, behold, there were none of the inhabitants of Jabeshgilead there. And the congregation sent thither twelve thousand men of the valiantest, and commanded them, saying, Go and smite the inhabitants of Jabeshgilead with the edge of the sword, with the women and the children."*

Jesus also confirmed this about what we do in such circumstances. Luke 11:23 says, *"He that is not with me is against me: and he that gathers not with me scatters."*

When we don't participate in the fight against sexual perversion, then it will affect our loved ones (who may be drawn into the same perversions sooner or later) and our families as it did with the families in Israel that never participated. Whatever the Lord has given you, should be dedicated in helping the cause of the Lord and the things that please Him.

Isaiah 56:4–5 says, *"For thus saith the LORD unto the eunuchs that keep my sabbaths, and choose the things that please me, and take hold of my covenant; Even unto them will I give in mine house and within my walls a place and a name better than of sons and of daughters: I will give them an everlasting name, that shall not be cut off."*

Mordecai mentioned to Esther the queen of the possibility that God brought her to that office of influence to help the Jews overcome their enemy. The same reason is valid to you, my reader. Esther 4:14 says, *"For if you altogether hold your peace at this time, then shall there enlargement and deliverance arise to the Jews from another place; but thou and thy father's house shall be destroyed: and who knows whether thou art come to the kingdom for such a time as this?"*

Finally, we need to support the witnesses who have escaped from sexual perversions so that they can withstand the temptations that the enemy might bring their way and pull them back.

Isaiah 16:4 says, *"Let mine outcasts dwell with thee, Moab; be thou a covert to them from the face of the spoiler: for the extortioner is at an end, the spoiler ceases, the oppressors are consumed out of the land."* Here we see God instructing us to help those who have survived the attacks of the spoiler (spirit of sexual perversion) using any resources within our reach.

When we do that, it will bring fruit to our spiritual accounts.

Philippians 4:15–17 says, *"Now ye Philippians know also, that in the beginning of the gospel, when I departed from Macedonia, no church communicated with me as concerning giving and receiving, but you only. For even in Thessalonica ye sent once and again unto my necessity. Not because I desire a gift: but I desire fruit that may abound to your account."*

Prayer

Father, in the name of Jesus, I repent supporting anything that you hate, including sexual perversions.

Lord, I ask you to take away every desire in my heart that is against righteousness with the blood of Jesus. Give me a new heart that takes pleasure in what you love.

Lord, I ask you to remove every curse from me, which has come as a result of me using your resources to enhance the kingdom of Satan.

Lord, open my eyes to see the needs of the kingdom and guide me to what I have to do to fight against sexual perversions using the influence and resources you have given me so that I may bear fruit. In Jesus's mighty name. Amen.

GRAND FINALE

In conclusion, we want to see some of the characteristics of the spirit of sexual perversion in Scripture. These can manifest spiritually in dreams and visions or physically in it's agents and victims.

A. Woman sitting on many waters – Revelation 17:1–2 says, *"And there came one of the seven angels which had the seven vials, and talked with me, saying unto me, Come hither; I will shew unto thee the judgment of the great whore that sits upon many waters: With whom the kings of the earth have committed fornication, and the inhabitants of the earth have been made drunk with the wine of her fornication."*

The spirit of sexual perversion is in the image of a woman who has infiltrated millions of people's lives and made them drunk on the wine of fornication. A drunk person gets their senses impaired, that s why, with this spirit in our lives, we may not differentiate between a grownup from a child, a person from an animal, a male from a female, a relative from a stranger, a physical body from a gadget, natural from unnatural. All these appear the same to us as potential sexual partners.

B. Sheds the saints' blood – Revelation 17:6 says, *"And I saw the woman drunken with the blood of the saints, and with the blood of the martyrs of Jesus: and when I saw her, I wondered with great admiration."*

This spirit is charged with shedding the blood of many Christians and servants of Jesus Christ, and it is out in the world, looking for more because it is obsessed with their blood as a delicacy.

C. Turns the heart away from God – Hosea 4:11 says, *"Whoredom and wine and new wine take away the heart."*

The spirit of sexual perversion, alcohol, and drugs (intoxication) have the same goal, which is to take away people's hearts from God without the victims realizing it. We can even stay in church, "Serve the Lord or do charitable works," but when our hearts are away from the master.

D. Brings a curse – Proverbs 6:32–33 says, *"But whoso commits adultery with a woman lacks understanding: he that doeth it destroys his own soul. A wound and dishonour shall he get; and his reproach shall not be wiped away."*

This spirit causes us to be dishonored at every level or status in life and brings a curse upon us that will cause persistent failure to happen in different areas of our lives.

E. Teaches ministers abominations – Revelation 2:20 says, *"Notwithstanding I have a few things against thee, because thou suffers that woman Jezebel, which calleth herself a prophetess, to teach and to seduce my servants to commit fornication, and to eat things sacrificed unto idols."*

This spirit teaches servants of God, whether kids or adults, how to fornicate without learning it from anyone. It disconnects them from the spirit of God and reconnects them to the spirit of false prophecy. And when they continue doing ministry they get the same manifestations (miracles, healings, financial breakthroughs, ministry opportunities) but, this time, from a different source(Satanic power).

F. Dresses up individuals – Proverbs 7:10 says, *"And, behold, there met him a woman with the attire of an harlot, and subtle of heart."*

This spirit has a strong garment it puts on our spirit, soul, or body and which controls our feelings and desires. Like a young child cannot undress themselves after being dressed by a superior person, so is the same for us. We have to call on Jesus Christ, who is more powerful than this spirit, to remove such spiritual garments from us with his blood.

G. Persists on her goal – Proverbs 7:11–12 says, *"She is loud and stubborn; her feet abide not in her house: Now is she without, now in the streets, and lieth in wait at every corner."*

This spirit is stubborn to the extent that it can pursue us through someone for years without giving up until we give in to its advances. It is also stubborn when it comes to casting it out of our lives. It will only surrender and leave when the spirit of God wears it out.

H. She masks up – Proverbs 7:13 says, *"So she caught him, and kissed him, and with an impudent face said unto him."*

This spirit puts an innocent, appealing, caring, or seductive mask on the people it uses to get into our lives. Because of this, we never see its claws. Only until we are trapped will the real character of a person be revealed.

I. She credits herself with hard work – Proverbs 7:15 says, *"Therefore came I forth to meet thee, diligently to seek thy face, and I have found thee."*

This spirit will deceive us that it has invested so much into getting our attention or lost so many opportunities just to get to us so that it may gain compassion from us.

J. Promises heaven on earth – Proverbs 7:16 says, *"I have decked my bed with coverings of tapestry, with carved works, with fine linen of Egypt."*

This spirit will promise us anything it thinks will excite us on any level attained so that, in pursuing the goodies, we are trapped and continue in its perversions until we die without ever being satisfied.

K. Protects us until the appointed day, – Proverbs 7:19–20 says, *"For the goodman is not at home, he is gone a long journey: He hath taken a bag of money with him, and will come home at the day appointed."*

This spirit will cover us up as we act on its perversions so that no one will know what is happening until at the appointed day it sets to shame us in public. It can keep a recorded video, picture, audio, or any proof of sexual perversion for decades until it sees an opportune time to show the world our nakedness.

L. Deposits words in the heart – Proverbs 7:21 says, *"With her much fair speech she caused him to yield, with the flattering of her lips she forced him."*

This spirit will use its agents to speak words into our hearts that will keep ringing due to its sweetness until they force us to yield to its suggestions. It can also give us seducing lips to win over whomever we talk to. This has caused many to return to perversion even after deliverance because they never asked the Lord to wash away those words and cut off those lips with his blood.

M. Blinds spiritual eyes – Proverbs 7:22 says, *"He goes after her straightway, as an ox goes to the slaughter, or as a fool to the correction of the stocks."*

This spirit blinds our eyes so that we invest our resources in things or people who are going to commit perversions in our lives.

Many people have brought house helps into their homes who have snatched away their spouses or molested their kids.

N. Switches great heritages – Proverbs 7:23 says, *"Till a dart strike through his liver; as a bird hastes to the snare, and knows not that it is for his life."*

This spirit causes us to sell our precious heritage (comparison: as a liver is to a body) to it as we indulge in sexual perversion, and when we should have gotten our blessing (finances, offspring, ministry, marriage), instead, we are disqualified. It shoots at our inheritance, puts it in a snare, and torments our lives.

O. It has paths – Proverbs 7:25 says, *"Let not thine heart decline to her ways, go not astray in her paths."*

This spirit has special paths it uses to get into our lives, which we must find out and block with the blood of Jesus to stop its activities.

P. Wounds hearts – Proverbs 7:26 says, *"For she hath cast down many wounded: yea, many strong men have been slain by her."*

This spirit causes wounds in our hearts, which it uses to cast down many strong people. Because of their wounds, men have hated women and resorted to liking their fellow men while women, likewise, have hated men and resorted to liking their fellow women. These wounds have to be washed away from our hearts with the blood of Jesus.

Q. Has a spiritually locked house – Proverbs 7:27 says, *"Her house is the way to hell, going down to the chambers of death."*

This spirit has a locked spiritual house where it keeps all its agents and victims. True deliverance can only be attained after we have spiritually broken out of that house. Angels can help us break out when we call them to our rescue. When we fail to break out of that house, then we would be finally transferred to the chambers of death.

INDEX